Little Hearts Books

Whispers Through Time
Communication Through the
Ages and Stages of Childhood

Best-selling parenting and children's book author, L.R.Knost, is an independent child development researcher and founder and director of the advocacy and consulting group, Little Hearts/Gentle Parenting Resources, as well as a monthly contributor to *The Natural Parent Magazine*. She is also a babywearing, breastfeeding, co-sleeping, homeschooling mother of six. Her children are a twenty-five-year-old Pastor and married father of two; a twenty-three-year-old married Family Therapist working on an advanced degree; an eighteen-year-old university pre-med student on scholarship; thirteen- and six-year-old sweet, funny, socially active, homeschooled girls; and an adorable twenty-five-month-old toddler. Other works by L.R.Knost include the first in the *Little Hearts Handbook* parenting guide series, *Two Thousand Kisses a Day: Gentle Parenting Through the Ages and Stages*, and her children's picture books, *A Walk in the Clouds,* the soon-to-be-released *Grumpykins* series, and *Petey's Listening Ears*, the first in the *Wisdom for Little Hearts* series, which are humorous and engaging tools for parents, teachers, and caregivers to use in implementing gentle parenting techniques in their homes and schools.

*Note: Information contained in this book is for educational purposes only and should not be construed as medical or mental health counsel.

Whispers Through Time
Communication Through the Ages and Stages of Childhood

L.R.Knost

A Little Hearts Handbook
Little Hearts Books, LLC. ▪ U.S.A.

Photography credit: Melissa Lynsay Photography and iStock

I wish you the sweetness of sticky kisses
the fragrance of muddy bouquets of weeds
the simplicity of macaroni necklaces
the warmth of bedtime snuggles
the promise of beautiful tomorrows...

I wish you the hope to carry your heart through hard times
the grace to forgive your inevitable mistakes
the strength to start again every morning
the wisdom to enjoy the journey...

I wish you enough joy and laughter in the present
to fill the silence that comes too soon
when life grows quiet
and rooms grow still
and your heart beats in constant prayer
for the once-small feet that now choose their own path
guided by the whisper of their childhood.

L.R.Knost

Table of Contents

Introduction

A Gentle Beginning

Toddler Time

A Preschooler with a Plan

Middle Childhood: Becoming Their Own Person

Gentle Parenting: Teens and Beyond

Appendix A

Appendix B

References

Chapter 1

Communication:
Whispers Through Time

Communication is the path to all human interaction. Whether it is a conversation, a book, an email, a text, a piece of art, a song, or just the quirk of an eyebrow, the objective is to connect with another soul, to share something of ourselves, or to ask for something to be shared with us. We may need information or guidance. We might want to share a thought or a message. Or we may simply need to know that someone is listening, someone hears, someone cares. Whatever the need, whatever the motivation, communication is the link between us and the world.

But communication can be downright difficult, especially when it's between people who are different from one another. Different languages, cultures, sexes, backgrounds, belief systems, and, certainly, different generations can all be roadblocks in the vital path of communication.

As humans we often hear only what we want to hear or what we think someone is going to say, or we get so focused on what we want to say next that we miss entirely what is actually being said.

And that is where communication fails. Communication traveling in only one direction and not being received, processed, and returned effectively leaves the 'commune' (sharing, connecting, bonding, interacting) out of communicate, rendering it at the very least useless, but more often damaging to the relationship. This can occur in parenting when communication breaks down, frustration overcomes reason, and parents react punitively to that frustration rather than pausing, listening, processing, understanding, and empathizing.

The thing is, though, if we as parents stop using violence and intimidation to control our children and instead work together with them through connection and communication, the adults we send into the world when they are grown are far more likely to be true world changers.

It's not our job to toughen our children up to face a cruel and heartless world. It's our job to raise children who will make the world a little less cruel and heartless. And it is communication, that sharing of thoughts and ideals, that meeting of hearts and minds, that human connection, that can accomplish that lofty goal.

When it comes to parent/child relationships, the onus is entirely upon the parent to facilitate effective communication. The relationship by its very definition is unequal in that children are entirely at their parent's 'mercy.' Childhood isn't a job that a child can quit. It isn't a class that can be dropped or a romantic relationship that can be broken with an "It's not you. It's me." Children can't stage sit-ins or protests or vote their parents out of office. They are, effectively, 'stuck' with what they were born or adopted into.

In every way, the parent/child relationship reflects the parents' mindset, whether that be kind, empathetic, and responsive; or distant, disconnected, and austere; or harsh, controlling, and punitive. Parents choose, day in and day out, the kind of home environment in which their children will grow up. Parents decide, every day, how their children will view the world. And parents impact, over and over again, who their children will grow up to be.

Communication is the core of all parent/child interaction. Whether parents choose to brandish it like a sword to control their children or wield it like a mallet to hammer their children into shape or whisper it like an invitation to follow, communication is the means of parenting. What is lacking in the sword and the mallet is connection, sharing, understanding, camaraderie…that 'commune' element of communication.

Parents who, instead, choose to whisper, "Come, join me and we'll walk through life together," are, in effect, joining hands with their children and growing together into a beautiful friendship that will last a lifetime.

So, come, join me as we walk through the ages and stages of childhood and discover what's normal for each developmental stage and how to effectively communicate with your child at every juncture along the path to adulthood.

Chapter 2

Baby Talk

Communication begins at the moment of birth. Interwoven in those precious moments after a newborn is placed on a mama's belly are the first cry, the first eye contact, the first rooting for the breast, and the first opportunity to respond, to meet needs, to connect.

The days and nights that follow spent adjusting to the newness of life, those first exhausting weeks trying to get into the rhythm of parenthood, the awe-filled moments and the awful moments, the sweet smiles and the heartbreaking cries, all offer the opportunity to establish a foundation of trust upon which you can build a healthy parent/child relationship.

Research has shown hints of the remarkable ability of newborns to communicate their needs.[1] From the moment they enter the world, babies are trying to communicate. Crying, grunting, making eye contact, mirroring expressions, rooting, cooing, and more are all the instinctive tools built into infants to reach out into a brand new world and make contact. These are amazing abilities, to be sure, but it is up to the parent to make the connection, to respond, to build those all-important 'lines of communication' that will be so vital in later childhood.

Communication is not something that just happens. It is not something that begins when a child becomes verbal, and it's not a product of a child's advancing maturity. Communication is a process, a relational building block, a result of intentional and responsive parenting.

Whether or not you feel that you can confidently distinguish between your baby's grunts and cries and cues for every need, the real message here is that staying tuned-in to your little one and offering immediate and loving attention are key to developing communication, security, and trust.

Here are some ideas about how to respond to your baby's attempts to communicate:

1. Crying is often called a 'late-stage' cue for hunger. Watching for hand chewing, rooting, lip-smacking, etc. will give you earlier cues to your baby's hunger so you can meet that need before your baby gets distressed.

2. Babies often get overwhelmed with too much noise and activity. Watch for signs your baby is getting overstimulated such as fussiness or turning their face away and give your little one a break from visiting relatives or overactive siblings or just the activity of normal life. You can step into a quiet room for a bit, take a little walk, or just put your baby in a sling or wrap and let them relax to the sound of your heartbeat.

3. Babies aren't mature enough to self-soothe. As parents, it's our job to soothe our little ones. Responding to your baby's whimpers or grunts before they reach the crying stage teaches them that they don't have to cry to have their needs met. When you hear a little squeak or rustle from your sleeping baby in the night or at naptime, watch and listen for a moment. If the sounds start to escalate, you can try patting their little bottom or rubbing their tiny back. If the escalation continues, pick your little one up and soothe them. Every need a baby communicates is valid, whether it's hunger or a diaper change or a cuddle, and our response communicates in return that they can count on us to meet their needs.

4. Tummy time is often uncomfortable for babies and babywearing can meet the same need for strengthening neck and core muscles. If your little one communicates their discomfort, don't ignore it or try to distract them. Respond by adjusting to their needs and try babywearing[2] instead.

5. Some babies adore bathtime while others find it traumatic. If your baby communicates distress, try lightly swaddling them and doing a sponge bath by uncovering one little body part at a time and washing and rinsing it instead of doing a tub bath. You can wait a few weeks and try the bath again later when your baby may be more comfortable with it.

The point of each of these ideas is to watch and listen to your baby's cues and respond quickly and appropriately to their unique needs. That back and forth, back and forth expression of needs and meeting of needs is the beginning of a lifetime of healthy communication skills and the basis of trust-based, gentle parenting!

Chapter 3

Becoming Mommy

"Parents aren't perfect people. They're people being perfected."

In the deep stillness of the night, a newborn's cry pierces the silence. A young mother, her body aching from the trial of giving birth, eases herself into a rocking chair with her precious new babe cradled in her arms. The gentle creak of untried wood settling into a life of service accompanies a soft-voiced lullaby as the baby's cries drift back to silence with a tiny sigh. Despite her exhaustion, the new mother smiles tenderly as she tends her baby's needs. And there, in that wooden rocking chair in the still of the night, a mommy is born.

There is great truth to the idea that it takes more than bringing a child into the world to be a parent. It is in the moments of sacrifice, the placing of another's needs before our own, the daily learning and evolving, the growth that only comes through time and experience and, yes, even failure, that a person becomes a parent.

The truth, paradoxical as it may seem, is that we become more of who we are by becoming less of who we were. It is in the letting go of self, that conception of identity that can so tie us down, that the depth and breadth of the human heart reaches its true potential.

In other words, and more specifically as a parent, embracing the new realities of our life with a precious new little life to care for and guide and protect and love doesn't make us lose ourselves. It gives us the chance to find more of ourselves, to delve more deeply into the richness of our potential, and to become more than we ever imagined possible.

Mommy or daddy, birth parent or adoptive parent, it doesn't matter who we are, what matters is who we are becoming. It's okay to let go of old conceptions of self; it's okay to dive headfirst into this new season of life; it's okay to let go of me to become we.

By not fighting this newness of life and instead embracing that new life, consciously and wholeheartedly, we will save ourselves and our children unnecessary struggle and angst and heartache. It all begins by communicating with our old selves that it's time to move on...

A new, breastfeeding mother stands in front of her bathroom mirror and holds a cold cloth against her cracked nipples. In the mirror she sees a different body than she used to see. This body with engorged breasts and a scattering of stretch marks is unfamiliar, but bears the signs of bringing new life into the world. The new mother may sigh over the loss of her pre-pregnancy body, but over time as she accepts these badges of motherhood, her heart grows beyond a narrow view of beauty to embrace the many forms of lovely femininity.

A young father nervously embarks on a trip to a foreign country to meet his son for the first time. The adoption process has been long and expensive, the emotional toll heavy. He moves aside as a man close to his age breezes by the economy seats on the plane on his way to first-class with his big-ticket suit perfectly pressed and the rich aroma of his cologne trailing behind him like a fawning lackey. The new father glances down at his jeans and slightly wrinkled button-up and grimaces, but as he sinks into his narrow coach seat, he pulls out a picture of his long-awaited son and smiles tenderly, his heart unconsciously broadening the meaning of success to include this arduous, rewarding pilgrimage into fatherhood.

Parenting is a journey that tries and tests us to the deepest, untapped parts of our souls. Embarking on parenthood with the understanding that life as we know it is over, that we will never be the same, and that that is exactly why it is so extraordinary and exhausting and powerful and perplexing and thrilling and terrifying and breathtaking and bewildering helps to prepare us for the remarkable journey ahead as we let go of who we were to become who we are meant to be.

Chapter 4

Baby Signing:
A Gentle Introduction to Communication

Most parents can relate to the frustration of trying to figure out what an adorable, roly-poly, much-loved, but non-verbal baby is trying to communicate with their sometimes incomprehensible babbles and inconsolable cries.

Wouldn't it be wonderful, though, if there was some way we could open the door for our babies to be able to communicate with us more effectively before they could even learn to talk? What if they could tell us when they were hungry or thirsty or tired or sad or scared without always having to resort to crying?

Gentle parenting is founded on trust created from responsiveness and empathy and built with connection and communication. But that can be a tall order when faced with a little one with exactly zero language skills and a vocabulary that consists of only babbling and crying.

Enter ~ the wonders of baby sign language.

Research[3] has shown that babies who learn just a few basic words using sign language tend to exhibit markedly less crying. As they grow into the early toddler stage, frustration-driven behaviors such as hitting and biting were also shown to be greatly reduced. It's not a surprising finding, though. Since the frustration caused by not being able to communicate is often at the root of tantrums and aggression in small children, it stands to reason that reducing that frustration would also reduce emotional outbursts.

What is amazing is the significant impact utilizing baby sign language has on parents and caregivers themselves. They reported less frustration on their own part when caring for babies who have learned how to express themselves with a few key words in sign language, and studies showed increased interactions between caregivers and babies, as well as improved responsiveness and empathy.

Perhaps even more remarkably, though arguably not as important to new, stressed out parents trying to be responsive to their baby's needs without always knowing specifically what those needs are, follow up research with children who were taught sign language as babies revealed a startling increase in language ability, vocabulary, and IQ compared to children who had not been taught signing as babies.

There are baby signing books and classes and even YouTube tutorials readily available that can teach the basic signs. So before you throw in the proverbial towel and end up crying in-tune with your little one, take a little foray into the world of baby signing and see if it helps you tune-in to them instead.

Some practical tips to help you get started:

1. Begin to introduce signs along with words and actions. For instance, when breastfeeding or bottle-feeding, demonstrate the word 'milk' while saying "milk," and when offering solids, demonstrate the word 'eat' while saying "eat," etc. Keep in mind that it can take several weeks or even months before babies begin to use the signs themselves, and even then it may a while before they use them consistently.

2. Some of the first words you may want to introduce, in addition to 'milk' and 'eat,' are 'mommy' and 'daddy' and 'more' and 'all-done' and 'diaper' and 'play.'

3. As with teaching your little one anything else, repetition and keeping it fun are key. Don't expect them to get new words right away or to remember to use signing all the time. Remember, when they get overwhelmed with upsets or excitement or are tired or sleepy or hungry they may fall back on their default communication--crying. That's okay. Sign language is merely a tool to help them communicate, not a cure for babyhood!

Chapter 5

The Power of Perception

On a recent trip to the park, I overheard a parent ranting and raving about a toddler "being a brat and always pitching fits." It took me less than two seconds of looking at the child to realize his mother had put him down on hot asphalt without shoes on, and his 'fit' was actually cries of pain as he danced around trying to keep his little feet off the asphalt while trying to push past his mommy to get back into the car. In a few years this mother will wonder why her ten-year-old is always so sullen and silent.

Later the same day in the grocery store, a three-year-old asked her mommy what plastic wrap was for. The mother rolled her eyes and snapped, "For wrapping food in plastic, duh." A few years from now, this mother will confess to a friend that she has no idea why her nine-year-old is so mouthy and rude.

Minutes later, a two-year-old riding past me in a shopping cart babbled in her cute baby language, looking at her daddy with a delighted smile. Her father ignored her first few attempts to get his attention, then finally barked, "Shut up!" without ever looking at her. In a few years this father will complain to his co-workers that his teenaged daughter never talks to him.

What's happening here? Are these isolated cases of bad parenting? Are these just bad parents? Or is something else at work?

While it's certainly possible that some people are just too self-absorbed or stressed or rushed to give their children the care and attention they need, often the problem lies in the parents' perceptions of their child. How often have you heard parents describe their children in terms such as these:

"My two-year-old is a little dictator."

"That kid is going to be a handful when she grows up."

"My newborn pitches a fit when I change him."

"Gotta go. The brat needs me."

"My six-month-old is so stubborn."

"Here comes trouble."

"She's spoiled rotten."

Instead of...

"My two-year-old is a little genius."

"That girl is going to be somebody special when she grows up."

"My newborn cries when I change him, poor little guy."

"Gotta go. My little one needs me."

"My six-month-old is so smart."

"Here comes my little man."

"My little lady knows what she needs."

Look at the contrast in descriptive phrases: little dictator, a handful, pitches a fit, brat, stubborn, trouble, spoiled rotten...little genius, somebody special, poor little guy, little one, smart, little man, little lady.

Let's face it, parents, we're human. And, as humans, we are far more likely to respond kindly to someone who we see in a positive light. No one likes to feel used or lied to or manipulated, and the words we use to characterize our children's behavior not only reveal what our feelings are toward our children themselves, but also strongly influence our responses to them.

Consider:

- A baby cries in the night. The parent who hears the cry as communicating a need will respond quickly and consistently. The parent who hears the cry as manipulation will likely ignore the cries.

- A toddler has a meltdown. The parent who sees a small child overwhelmed by big emotions and unable to articulate his needs will respond with empathy. The parent who sees a stubborn little dictator pitching a fit because he didn't get his own way will typically ignore or punish the toddler.

- A preschooler complains of a stomach ache every morning before being dropped off at daycare. The parent who hears a vulnerable child with limited language skills trying, in the only way she can, to express the loneliness and anxiety she feels at the daily separation will respond with understanding and comfort. The parent who hears a lie and feels manipulated will likely react with anger or impatience.

- A child comes home from school and has a meltdown when asked if he has any homework. The parent who sees a little person overwhelmed and struggling will respond with compassion and assistance. The parent who sees a lazy spoiled brat will typically react with threats and demands.

- A teenager screams, "You don't understand me!" The parent who hears the hurt and need behind the words will stop talking and start listening. The parent who hears rebellion and disrespect will likely respond with anger or a lecture.

Parents around the world and across the ages have heard a baby's cry, coped with a toddler's meltdown, dealt with a child's anger, and faced an adolescent's attitude, and in each and every case the motivation that the parents attributed to the behavior has been the single most powerful determinant in the parents' response.

But the impact of the parents' perception is even more powerful than just a momentary appropriate or inappropriate response. The parents' perceptions all too often become the reality. In other words, who they believe they are raising is who they will raise.

Here's the thing, if you call a child a liar often enough, they will become deceptive. If you treat a child like they are manipulating you often enough, they will become conniving. If you label a child a spoiled brat, they will become impudent and rebellious.

By the same token, if you treat a child like a priceless gift, handling them with care and respect, they will grow up valuing themselves and others.

Parents, your relationship with your teenager is being established now, while your child is still a toddler. Your discipline issues with your nine-year-old are being minimized or intensified right now, while he is reaching out to you in infancy. Preschooler's tantrums are being moderated or exacerbated at this moment by your response or lack of response to your baby's cries.

So, who are you raising, parents? An innocent child or a cunning manipulator? It's vital that you decide, because your perception of who your child is and what motivates them will influence not only your attitude toward your child, but your response to your child as well.

Remember, who you think you are raising is who you will raise!

Chapter 6

Eleven Tips to Beat the Weary Dreary Mama Blues

Mountains of laundry. Piles of toys. Diapers and dishes and dust. Sticky fingerprints to wipe. Muddy shoeprints to mop. Bills to pay. Appointments to keep. Shopping to do...

The parenting list is endless because 'done' doesn't exist in a world where little ones live and play and grow. But parents are people, too, and we can get overwhelmed at the sheer redundancy of the cycle of life with children if we don't intentionally take the time to feel the joy of little arms wrapped around our necks and to find something of ourselves in the busyness of daily life. If you're on the verge of losing the battle of the blues, here are eleven ways to energize, prioritize, and conceptualize your way back to a healthier, happier you!

1. *Go outside. No joke.* Taking your problems and frustrations outside shrinks them down like shrinky-dinks in an oven. When you've got the warm sun on your face and you're watching your little ones tumbling in the green grass and you're listening to giggles replace their whines, life feels good again.

2. *Write it down to turn your frown upside-down.* Seriously, writing down a list of all the good things in your life in one column and the bad things in another helps to restore a healthy perspective.

3. *Go to the dark side!* Take a good look at the bad things on your list and see what you can do to cross off or minimize some of the things on the bad side. Sometimes just eliminating one sore point or reducing one stressor can make a world of difference!

4. *It's okay to have a disposable day.* Take one day a week and use paper plates and plastic cups and utensils to give yourself a chance to catch up on those pesky dishes. It's okay. Really.

5. *The Earl of Sandwich invites you to dine.* Another way to beat the dishes doldrums is to have a sandwich day. Egg sandwiches for breakfast. Peanut butter and jelly sandwiches for lunch. Turkey sandwiches for dinner. And who really needs to have a plate to lay their sandwich on, anyway? A paper towel will do for a plate and a napkin all in one!

6. *A load a day keeps the mountain away.* Doing one load of laundry every day instead of storing it up for a huge 'laundry day' once a week is one way to tame the daunting mountain into a doable molehill.

7. *Spray the stickies away.* Little people usually love spray bottles or water guns, so harness that love for some rock 'em sock 'em cleaning help. Put a pair of daddy's white sports socks on little feet and little hands and arm your small ones with a bit of water in a spritzer or water gun, then join them for an all-out blitz on fingerprints, dust bunnies, and jelly smears!

8. *There can never be too many cooks in the kitchen.* The littlest member of the family can be worn in a baby carrier while the cook cooks or the cleaner cleans. For tinies who are a bit bigger, instead of barring them from the kitchen, turn them into little sous-chefs and let them measure and sort and stir. If they're too little for actual cooking, put pots and pans and measuring bowls on the floor with a bit of sudsy water so they can whip up a storm while you're cooking or cleaning. Afterward, scooch some towels across the floor with your feet for a bit of exercise and a semi-cleaned floor as a bonus!

9. *And speaking of exercise, get some of that groovy stuff.* Doing knee bends while you brush your teeth, lunges while vacuuming and babywearing, and boogying with your children to some funky music while straightening can all contribute to a mood-lifting, age-defying, endorphin-releasing surge of healthy goodness while weaving in some far out fun!

10. *Daydreamer, dream on.* Don't forget that you're a one-of-a-kind, never-before-seen, gift-to-the-world, and you've got a super-special purpose for being here. Raising your children is an amazing and wonderful privilege, but you'll have a lot of life left to live once your children are out of the early stages of intense need for your time and attention. So take a few moments every day to dream those dreams while staring out the window over a steaming cup of coffee, and journal those thoughts and ideas and plans. Your time will come, mama!

11. *Don't forget the chocolate!* Everyone likes to be appreciated, and a sweet reward at the end of the day says "Good job" like few other things can. So stash some luscious dark chocolate next to a good book and escape the joyful chaos of life with littles for a few minutes every evening after everyone's asleep and the still-messy house lies quiet and still. The mess will be there in the morning, but the quiet moment won't. Relax, mama. You deserve it!

Underestimating the effect of exhaustion and unmet needs on your parenting is a common mistake that can lead to unintentional negative responses toward your children. As a result, your parenting can get so crowded with these unconscious reactions that your good intentions get lost. Just as a child's behavior can reveal their underlying unmet needs, a parent's knee-jerk reactions can reveal hidden needs and hurts that surface with stress or frustration.

When reaction has overtaken intention in your parenting, take the time to identify and work through your unmet needs and unforgiven hurts; equip yourself with the tools to handle behavioral challenges with connection and communication; and don't forget to take time for fun and relaxation.

Becoming a peaceful and effective parent takes conscious effort, patience, and grace, not only toward your children, but toward yourself, as well!

~ Toddler Time ~

Chapter 7

*The Taming of the Tantrum:
A Toddler's Perspective*

A toddler speaks...

So parents, here's the scoop on tantrums:

They're your fault.

Okay, okay, so maybe my toddlerhood contributes to them a teensy-weensy bit, but seriously...

You, with the obsession with brushing teeth and bedtimes and matching clothes, enough already! Does it ever even occur to you that there's another person (Yes, I am an actual separate person from you. Remember that whole cutting of the umbilical cord thing?) who might have an opinion about what goes in my mouth or when I'm tired or not or what I want to wear?

And you, the one who thinks carrots and kale are food. Really? You have all kinds of opinions about what tastes good and what doesn't, but I'm not allowed to have any?

And don't even get me started on the rush-rush, hurry-up craziness that has me being snatched up in the middle of my most fantastic block tower ever and strapped into a torture device (Btw, where's your *carseat?!?) and dragged from one place to another right through snack time. I can't have an agenda? Don't my interests mean anything?*

Okay, so maybe I don't know everything yet, but how am I going to learn if you just force these issues instead of communicating with me about things? That whole learning by osmosis thing (a.k.a. passive learning) didn't work for you in college, and it won't work with me, either.

You keep going on and on and ooooon about wanting me to listen. "Why won't you listen?" "If you'd listen for once!" "Would you just listen to me?!?" I've got three words for you...

Two. Way. Street.

Maybe instead of that whole failed learning by osmosis experiment you keep trying (You do know the definition of insanity is doing the same thing over and over again expecting a different result, right? Okay, okay, just checking!) you could read the research and find out that I learn by active engagement (two-way conversation!) and imitation. Yep, that's right. I learn from what you do, not just what you say.

So here's the deal...

Want me to learn to listen? Then listen to me. *Listen and respond to my cries when I'm a baby. Listen and reply to my babbling attempts at talking when I'm a toddler. Listen to my whining and respond patiently when I'm a preschooler. (I know it's annoying, but whining is my last step, kind of like your 'last nerve' you complain I'm stomping on, before I have a meltdown. It's my last-ditch effort to hold on to the tiny bit of self-control I've learned so far in my short life!) Listen and actually pay attention (a.k.a eye contact!) to my endless stories about snails when I'm in middle childhood and to my endless complaints and dramas when I'm in my teen years.*

Want me to learn respect? Then show me respect. *Show me that you respect my personal space by explaining the things you're doing to me like changing my diaper or strapping me into a carseat. Show me that you respect others by not talking about them behind their backs (Yes, I can and do hear you!) or yelling at them on the road. Show me that you respect my opinions by asking for them and accommodating them when you can. (I know you won't always be able to, but the times you do will help me to accept the times you can't.)*

Want me to learn compassion? Then show me compassion. *Respond kindly and gently when I'm upset or angry or just out-of-sorts. Stay close when my emotions overwhelm me and I have a meltdown moment. (I need your presence and compassion the most when I seem to deserve it or even want it the least!) And model compassion by treating others kindly in front of me.*

Want me to learn self-control? (This is a big one!) Then show me self-control. *Take a parental time-out when you get tired or overwhelmed or angry so I learn how to handle those big emotions. Count to ten and take some deep breaths instead of yelling or hitting. And pace yourself in this big world. I need to learn that it's okay to take care of myself and not feel like I have to fill every moment with plans and schedules and agendas. I'll learn that from watching you choose wisely from the many opportunities and pressures life will offer.*

Okay, so to wrap this up. My tantrums don't just come out of nowhere. They are the result of tiredness, hunger, frustration, anger, etc. You can prevent them, or at least minimize them, by keeping me fed and rested, by paying attention to my preferences, interests, and attempts to communicate, and by communicating kindly and patiently with me about upcoming changes or things I might not like. And keep in mind, I'm always watching and absorbing everything that goes on around me, so make sure you're living what you want me to learn!

Chapter 8

The NO Zone

The life of a small child is comprised of a daily onslaught of tempting surfaces begging for the artistry of a crayon, tall places crying out to be scaled, lovely little objects in need of a mouth or nose to visit, and dozens of other alluring glass and liquid and sharp things to be explored through the physics of gravity, the kinetics of concoctions, and the application of Newton's Laws of Motion. There is only one force powerful enough to defeat this nearly irresistible call of adventure, imagination, and discovery...*the No!*

Every child knows the power of *the No* to circumvent the most well-laid plans. Even tiny babies just weeks into the world are introduced to its power when they grasp a fistful of hair while nursing or reach for some lovely, squishy stuff while getting a diaper change. That itty bitty two-letter word is packed with a force beyond comprehension to a toddler, and when they finally figure out how to wrap their little lips around those letters and form the word "NO!" themselves, the possibilities seem limitless!

Do you want a cookie? *"No!"...Well, actually, yes, but how cool is it that when I said "No!" I controlled whether or not someone gave me a cookie!*

Do you want Daddy to hold you? *"No!" Well, yes, but I got to decide whether someone held me or not for a change!*

Do you want to play outside? *"No!" Actually, I do, but do I really get to decide for myself where I go? Cool!*

That kind of power and control can go to a little person's head, for sure! And the change in the big people when the word is used against them clearly demonstrates its incredible value. Their faces go from happy to serious or even angry, and sometimes a little person can even make a big person yell. What dazzling power!

And then when little ones manage a few more words in their vocabulary, they can add direct quotes from the most powerful beings they know ~ mommy and daddy. Quotes like, *"I said 'No'!"* and *"Don't you tell me 'No'!"* and *"No means 'No'!"*

The authority! The dominion! The clout! And using them against those powerful beings, watching them turn red in the face and yell and threaten...*well, it's a little scary and makes a small person feel really disconnected and upset*...but the surge of intense pleasure at feeling powerful and in control almost makes them feel like a big person for a moment!

And that's what they most long to be, just like mommy and daddy ~ big and strong and smart and powerful.

So what's a mommy or daddy to do when confronted with *the No* from their little power-mongers? First, take a deep breath, and then engage those adult brains.

What inherent power is there, really, in a little two-letter word? Only the power we give it! What if, instead of that tiny word being able to push our buttons, we just disconnected the buttons entirely and didn't react to *the No* at all? It would simply become a no, just another word to celebrate our precious little people adding to their fledgling vocabularies.

What if we backed up even further and disenfranchised *the No* from the beginning? When our newborn baby's flailing hands caught a tiny fistful of hair, what if we just smiled and gently removed it and kissed those itty bitty little fingers?

When our intrepid little explorers discovered the wonders of kitchen cabinets, what if we used cabinet locks but left one or two full of pots and pans and plastic bins for them to discover?

What if when our little people headed for the walls to do their best Michelangelo interpretation on them, we simply intercepted them and offered alternative canvases?

Or what if when they ascended the kitchen cabinets, we just scooped them up and headed outdoors for some climbing adventures?

The thing is, *the No* is only *the No* when we, the adults, make it *the No*. And it can become simply a no when we get creative and interactive and stop using a tiny two-letter word like it has "Phenomenal Cosmic Power in an itty-bitty living space!" (Aladdin 1994)[4]

Chapter 9

The Secret of the Whisper

If a picture is worth a thousand words, then a whisper is worth two thousand when it comes to parenting. In the same way that the instinctive human reaction to someone raising their voice is to raise our voice one octave higher, to out-shout the shouter, to over-power the person powering-up on us, the instinctive human response to someone whispering is to quiet down, to lean-in, to listen.

As parents, it's up to us to exercise the wisdom and maturity to control our own instinctive reaction to our children's piercing screams, ear-shattering shrieks, and mind-blowing, foot-stomping, out-of-control fits. Small people have big emotions and need help processing them. Their cries as babies and shrieks and tantrums as toddlers and meltdowns as preschoolers are, literally, cries for help.

Ignoring or punishing them, or reacting with anger ourselves, simply forces them to bury their unresolved emotions and causes us to miss an opportunity to not only share our wisdom by helping them process their big feelings, but also to guide our children toward more appropriate ways to communicate as they grow. In some cases, when a child's emotions are forced underground it results in a child who simmers with hidden rage just waiting to explode again or, worse, the rage may turn inward and result in a child who is withdrawn, detached, or even depressed.

Having parenting tools ready and waiting for the inevitable challenges of raising little humans is wise. When emotions begin running high, and as parents we can feel our own stress levels rising, knowing we have a well-stocked parenting toolbox with tried and tested tools helps us to keep our cool so that we can parent more intentionally and effectively.

In the first weeks of life, a baby has one 'default' mode of verbal communication...crying. They may give physical cues to their needs such as chewing on their hands to indicate hunger or the beginning of teething, but their verbal communication takes the sole form of crying.

From those first tiny squeaks and mewls of a newborn, a baby's cries mature into whimpers, squeals, screams, and sobs, all communicating one thing: *"I need help."* When we respond to our baby's cries quickly and gently, whether it's to feed them or change them or give them a cuddle, we communicate in return, *"I'm here. You can count on me."*

But then there are those times when we've fed them, changed them, burped them, rocked and cuddled and walked with them, and their piercing screams still shatter the silence...and our hearts. Those are times when parents often begin to feel overwhelmed, stressed, sometimes even resentful and angry because no matter what they try, they can't 'fix' their baby and make them stop crying. It is in those moments of frustration and distress that we need to breathe in deeply to calm ourselves, then stop stressing over trying to 'fix' our baby and instead whisper in our little one's ear, *"I'm here. I've got you. We'll get through this together."* They may not understand our words, but they will hear our heart.

The truth is that a baby's cries can't always be 'fixed' and sometimes the need they're communicating is the need to express their emotions, but they always, always need the comfort and assurance that they will be heard and that their needs will be met and that they can trust us to be there for them, no matter what.

Once a baby reaches the crawling, exploring, discovering stage, they often have a great time experimenting with the volume, pitch, and range of their voice, much to the chagrin of their parents and pretty much everyone else within earshot. The ear-shattering squeals and bellows and joyful shrieks at this stage can be disconcerting to us parents, to say the least, especially when our little falsetto performs their operatic interpretation in public places such as doctor's offices, libraries, and restaurants.

This is a prime opportunity to exercise the power of the whisper. When the first shriek splits the silence, we can hold our finger to our lips, smile like we're inviting them to join in on a secret, and whisper, *"It's whisper time. Let's use our little voices together."* Making a game out of it invites cooperation rather than demands obedience, a much more effective parenting technique, and practicing little voices together demonstrates what we want our little one to do instead of simply telling them what we don't want them to do.

Don't be surprised if it takes many repetitions over several outings before your little one begins to get the idea, though. As with all parenting, time and patience and an awareness (and acceptance!) of what is normal for each developmental stage is key.

Toddlers and preschoolers are famous for their big tantrums sparked by big emotions and big frustrations. Obviously being aware of and avoiding tantrum triggers such as hunger, tiredness, and over-stimulation is important. But even with the most proactive parenting, there may still be times when our little ones have unexpected, incomprehensible, inconsolable tantrums.

When faced with a toddler or preschooler in the throes of a tantrum, if we know what caused the tantrum, we can validate the emotion with a soft-voiced, *"You're angry (disappointed, sad, hurt) because you (fill in the blank)."* Often just hearing their feelings put into words is enough to calm a toddler who is frustrated at their inability to express themselves, but sometimes they need a bit of time and support to work through their big emotions.

If the tantrum continues we need to stay calm and present and remember that we are modeling self-control and self-regulation when we practice those skills instead of having an adult-style tantrum in response to our child's tantrum. Instead of trying to control our child's outburst with demands or threats or bribes, we can simply stay close and whisper, *"I hear you. I'm here."*

The secret of the whisper in taming a tantrum can be seen in the difference between dumping a bucket of water on a fire, which can force the fire underground where it may smolder and reignite unexpectedly, versus spraying a gentle mist on the fire so it's slowly and fully extinguished, leaving the ground saturated so the fire won't reignite. Settling your little one quietly and patiently with a whisper is the gentle mist that saturates them with your unconditional love and support so they don't simmer with hidden rage that may erupt spontaneously again.

Remember, no matter the problem, kindness is always the right response. When your child is having a problem, stop, listen, then respond to the need, not the behavior. The behavior can be addressed later, after the need has been met, because only then is the door to effective communication truly open.

The thing to keep in mind is that there is no cure for childhood. There is no parenting secret that will 'work' to keep children from being children. Children will cry. They will tantrum. They will yell and giggle and climb and run and throw things and build things and hit and hug and explore and make glorious mistakes and incredible discoveries. They will be human. They will be children. And that's more than okay. That's beautiful, messy, wonderful childhood, just as it should be.

Parents are guides through the incredible journey of childhood, not to keep their children from experiencing childhood, but to keep them safe as they learn the magnificent life lessons that childhood has to offer.

Chapter 10

*Ten Ways to Play
When Play is the Last Thing on your Mind*

Let's be honest. Parents are adults, and not every adult is
comfortable sitting on the floor playing with stuffed animals for
hours at a time. We don't always eagerly jump in puddles or
make mud-pies. We often have heavy things weighing on
us…health issues, financial strains, layoffs threatening, marital
conflict…and playing is the very last thing on our minds.

But the reality that play is the language of childhood and that our
children need us to connect with them on their terms is also on
our minds. The truth that childhood is such a brief season of life
and if we blink too long we'll miss this precious time with our
children just adds to the weight we carry, making playing with
them seem like another burden, another demand on our already
stretched-too-thin time, attention, and patience.

The thing is, though, that our children do need us to connect
with them in play. It's in the simplicity of play that children sort
through the complexity of life and, like puzzle pieces, put it all
together to make sense of the world. Play is how they process
the overwhelming task of acclimating to a big, strange,
sometimes scary world, and they need to feel securely connected
to us and in close communication with us as they find their way.
Play provides that connection and builds those oh-so-important
channels of communication that are essential in a healthy
parent/child relationship.

That, of course, leaves us in the dichotomous position of our
needs versus our children's needs, which in and of itself is not
conducive to a healthy relationship. So what's a busy,
overburdened, stressed parent to do?

Enter, the playful parent who weaves humor into the humdrum, tummy tickling into the routine, dancing into the dreary, and silliness into the mundane.

Need some ideas to get you started? Here are ten simple ways to weave playful parenting into the ordinary moments of everyday life:

1. When your baby is an infant, babywearing is the secret to playful connection and communication building. Wearing your baby close to your heart, singing and swaying and placing soft kisses on a tiny head while doing dishes and sweeping the floors and taking the dog for walks is a lovely, low-stress way to weave playfulness into your day.

2. When your baby is a bit older, continue wearing him as long as you both are comfortable with it because riding high on your hip or back lets him see the world from your vantage point and offers everyday moments to play with bubbles in the sink as you wash dishes, to dance through the house as you put away laundry, and to giggle together as you grocery shop.

3. Daily routines offer awesome opportunities to play as you 'tickle' your little one's teeth instead of brush them, 'capture' wild shoes that try to escape when you're leaving the house, and gently 'wrestle' with your little pajama monster before bed.

4. Wrangling a reluctant child into the carseat is often a dreaded and dreadful task. Try making a game out of it by tickling a little tummy while you buckle up straps or blowing some bubbles to distract your little one or making up a silly buckle-up song to ease the transition.

5. While driving, turn off the radio and make up silly stories or songs or simply talk about where you're going or what you see as you drive.

6. Reading to your little one from birth onward is the single best way to raise a reader. Make it more interactive by acting out the story, using different voices to read, and letting your child guess what's going to happen on each page before you read it.

7. Getting out the door in the morning can be a challenge. Turn it into a real challenge by having hopping contests to the car. Let your little one win and give tickle-kisses as their prize!

8. Bathtime is a great time for fun. Set sail to distant shores with your little pirate and search for hidden treasure, or go on a safari and find jungle animals floating in piles of bubbles, or go spelunking and make cave drawings on the sides of the tub with bath crayons.

9. As your children get older, their need for playful connection and communication is still strong. Play word games in the car. Turn math homework into playtime by using manipulatives to help them work things out. Cook together while singing pop tunes. Arm wrestle at the dinner table. Have a quick pillow fight in the morning to put everyone's grumpies to sleep.

10. Chores are a real chore. Try turning them into a game, instead! Get out a board game with dice and every time someone rolls they not only move their game piece, but pick up the same number of toys and put them away and then race back in time for their next turn.

The central idea here is to intentionally weave fun and play and connectedness and communication into your everyday moments to turn ordinary days into extraordinary memories that will last a lifetime!

Chapter 11

A Listening Heart

"Listening is where love begins." Fred Rogers

Often the first question parents ask when seeking parenting guidance is, "How can I get my child to listen?" There's a wealth of frustration in those words that parents everywhere can understand and empathize with, but there are deeper questions that need to be asked before that one can be answered. The first question is *"How, exactly, do you as a parent define listening?"* The second is *"What do you believe is the purpose of listening?"* Finally, and perhaps most importantly, *"How well do you, yourself, listen?"*

Take a moment before continuing to read and think about your definition of listening. Keep that definition, the one you've been operating from as a parent, in mind as you read on:

Listening is defined as *to pay attention to, to take notice of, to receive.*

Colloquially, though, and certainly in parenting, the word listening is often used to mean *to heed, to acknowledge, to obey.* Those meanings, however, are actually responses to listening rather than listening itself. What parents are typically asking when they say, *"How can I get my child to listen?"* is *"How can I get my child to obey?"*

Now think about times in your life when you didn't feel heard, whether it was in your own childhood, or in an adult relationship, your work environment, or another area of your life. How did that make you feel? Did you feel hurt? Unimportant? Dismissed? Misunderstood? Ignored? Examine those feelings and see if they bear any similarity to how you feel when your child doesn't appear to be listening to you. Ask yourself what that says about your need to be heard by your child. Is it obedience you're seeking or something deeper? Could your strong reaction to your child not listening to you be evidence of your own unmet needs or hurts from your past or present relationships?

Often the key to communication problems in parent/child relationships lies in the parent first working toward resolving their own hurts and finding ways of meeting their own needs. Once the parent has reached a place of peace in their own heart, they are able to focus on bringing that peace to their parenting. Listening can then become a mutual interaction, a means of communication and connection instead of being a source of conflict and a trigger for a negative parental emotional reaction.

Finally, take a moment and honestly ask yourself how well you, yourself, listen to your child. Remember, children learn best by imitation. What are you teaching them by your own example? Do you maintain eye contact with your child when they tell you their endless stories about lizards or superheroes or rocks? Do you let them explain why they need four bandages for an invisible scrape or why they can't possibly go to bed wearing purple pajamas? Do you give them your full attention when they speak, or are your thoughts occupied with what you want to say next or how you're going to make them obey? Do you insist that they listen to you first, that they hear and understand your point of view, before you're willing to listen to their viewpoint or explanation or problem?

For effective communication to take place, both parties need to hear the other. If both are focused on trying to be heard at the same time, neither will end up being heard. As the only adult in the parent/child relationship, it's up to you to listen first, to understand first, to acknowledge and validate your child first. You have the maturity and self-control to be patient and wait to be heard. Your child doesn't, especially when emotions are running high.

The reality is that parents who don't really listen to their children tend to have children who really don't listen to their parents. The flipside is that children whose parents listen to them, children who feel heard, tend to listen better to their parents.

That's not the end of it, though. Once parents have resolved their own issues with needing to feel heard and are working on modeling good listening to their children, there's the issue of the children's own immature listening skills to address. The modeling of those skills by parents in and of itself is a powerful teacher, but parents can facilitate their children's learning by identifying specific areas their children seem to have the most trouble with when it comes to listening and communication.

There are three components of verbal communication: listening, processing, and responding.

Listening is the first step in effective communication. If there is a problem at this level, it may be that your child doesn't feel heard or it may be an attention issue or a language issue. Listening, as mentioned earlier, is defined as *to pay attention to, to take notice of, to receive*…all meanings that also apply to the idea of connection. Solutions to these issues are, therefore, connection-based. Working on being in-tune with your child will help you to discern whether they don't feel heard, in which case you can intentionally reconnect with them and focus on actively listening to them, or if you need to eliminate distractions when communicating with them so they can more easily focus their attention on you, or if you need to work on finding more age-appropriate language to express yourself.

Processing is the next step in effective communication. Problems at this level can be difficult to discern because they are internal to the child as the child attempts to interpret what's been said and decide on an appropriate response. If your child seems to be attentively listening in the first step in communication, but struggles and gets stuck in the processing step, it can simply be a sign that you need to back up and try a different approach in the listening step and help them to receive the message you're trying to convey. Rarely, though, it can be a sign of a processing disorder such as attention-deficit disorder, auditory processing disorder, or other processing issues that may need to be evaluated.

Note: If you have any concerns about your child's communication skills or believe there may be a communication delay, having a professional evaluation sooner rather than later is a good idea. Discovering any issues, learning how to accommodate your child's communication needs, and starting appropriate early interventions can make a world of difference for your child and your relationship.

The last step in effective communication is responding. It is here that parents' true issues with their child's listening tend to reveal themselves. Parents who want their child to comply with requests or obey commands without question or delay will, themselves, have the most issues with this step.

Ideally, a child's response in most situations should be considered and thoughtful. A child needs to feel free to ask for explanations so that they can learn about their parents' thought processes. A child who feels confident enough to respond with questions and even alternative suggestions opens the communication channel to an exchange of ideas, desires, and needs on both sides and leads to a more cooperative parent/child relationship.

Parents who are focused on control often find the idea of an interactive response rather than instant, unquestioning obedience from their child to be an uncomfortable concept. It's in that exchange of thoughts, though, that children learn how an adult thinks and that they begin to internalize the belief systems and values parents ultimately want their children to take into adulthood.

Identifying where the breakdown in communication with your child occurs, whether it's in your own visceral response because of unmet needs, or it's in the listening step, the processing step, or the responding step, will help you to make whatever changes are necessary. Don't feel that you have to minutely analyze every interaction or conversation with your child, but instead pay attention to the overall atmosphere of communication in your relationship and be ready to step in and make adjustments as needed.

As your child grows and their grasp of language expands, your communication approach will need to evolve to meet their changing needs and abilities. The one thing that won't ever change, though, is the need to listen, really *listen* to your child.

I love the quote, *"Listening is where love begins,"* from Fred Rogers, best known for his PBS television show, *Mister Rogers' Neighborhood*, but I would add that, in parenting as in all relationships in life, *'Listening is where listening begins.'*

~ A Preschooler with a Plan ~

Chapter 12

A Child's Heart

As our family celebrated a birthday at a local ice cream shop, a scene unfolded in another booth that caught our attention. All of us quieted and watched, our hearts hurting for one little girl and touched by another as a clearly stressed-out parent lost her temper and her self-control.

It started as a little girl of about four or five tried to tell her mother what she wanted to order. Her mother didn't understand what she wanted, and the little girl became increasingly agitated and began to whine in frustration as she continued to try and fail to express herself. Finally the mother, also frustrated, grabbed the small girl by the arm and yanked her out of line and stomped over to the booth next to ours. She leaned over the now-crying child, yanked her face close to hers, and shouted, *"I have no idea what you want! I can't understand you! Why don't you just say what you want? Calm down! NOW!"*

My children looked at me, wide-eyed, knowing that I would gently intervene if things escalated as they've seen me do a number of times in the past. But something beautiful happened in that moment that none of us will ever forget. The little girl's sister, no older than eight or nine herself, stepped between her mother and sister and softly said, *"She wants vanilla, mom. That's all. When she said, 'Just the white,' that's what she meant. She just wants vanilla ice cream. That's all. It's okay, mom."*

The mother took a deep breath and blew the hair out of her face, then silently walked away to go order their ice cream. And as we watched, the older sister reached out, put her hands on either side of her little sister's face, and leaned over to softly kiss her on the top of the head.

I get it. We're human. We make mistakes. And I don't know what was going on in that stressed-out mother's life. But I do know this. There were two frustrated people in that situation, one an adult, one a small child. And it was the adult who lost it. It was the adult who stomped her feet and shouted and lashed out physically and verbally.

But it was a child who stepped in with a calm and understanding (and, unfortunately it appeared, practiced) response and brought peace back to the situation. It was a child who communicated, connected, and responded rather than reacting.

I hope and pray that the mother was just having a bad day, that the older sister, instead of having to step up and become a miniature adult in a household of immature adults as some children must do, was simply emulating what she'd seen her mother do on other occasions.

We're all capable of doing what that child did, of practicing understanding, of speaking peace. If a child has the presence of mind to address heightened emotions with quiet resolve and calm communication, then as adults we have no excuse for not doing the same.

Chapter 13

Why Whining is a Win

It's seven o'clock and you're finishing up the dishes before starting bedtime baths. And then it starts…the whining. Every. Single. Night. Your four-year-old knows the routine. She knows you are going to read her favorite bedtime book. She knows you will let her choose which pajamas to wear. She knows she has to brush her teeth. But that doesn't stop her from standing in the kitchen night after night whining about the same things.

So what's the deal? Short-term memory loss? An innate desire to drive you crazy? A disorder of the vocal cords that makes using a normal voice impossible after the sun sets and every time she doesn't get her way *all day long*?!?

Here's a shocker for you: Whining is actually a sign of maturity! Yep, that unnerving, endless, nails-on-a-chalkboard, make-your-head-explode whine is a sign that your little one is growing up and, get this, gaining self-control! I can see your heads shaking, but read on, parents, caregivers, and bleeding ears of the world, read on.

Whining, believe it or not, is an advanced skill. Babies come into the world with exactly one form of verbal communication-- crying. They may smack their lips and root for the breast when hungry. They may arch their back or wiggle in discomfort when they need a diaper change. But when physical expressions don't result in needs being met or their needs are emotional rather than physical, then crying is always the 'default' communication. Every need, every discomfort, every bit of loneliness or anxiety or frustration or stress has to be communicated through that one single venue.

Over time as babies grow into toddlers, they begin to learn new ways to communicate, pointing, grunting, picking up a few words here and there, and they move into a more interactive stage wherein they make attempts to communicate in these new ways, but fall back very quickly into crying if they aren't understood and responded to quickly.

As time goes on, toddlerhood gives way to the preschool years and language skills advance, becoming the main source of communication for a little one. But even so, their grasp of language is limited and their prefrontal cortexes (center of forethought/pre-thinking skills) are still developing. This leads to a rather dichotomous situation in which they know what they want to say, but often can't quite put the words together quickly or clearly enough for us oh-so-impatient adults.

As they work to communicate, their frustration levels rise and stress hormones sap the blood flow from those underdeveloped 'thinking' portions of their brains and, just when they need the use of language the most, they begin to lose the ability to articulate their needs. As toddlers they would fall quickly back into crying at this point, but as preschoolers their more advanced self-control helps them to avoid immediately dissolving into tears and, instead, they fall into the 'middle-ground' of whining.

Whining is, in fact, just an advanced form of crying and, as such, is just as grating on the nerves as crying because it is designed to get the attention of a caregiver. The difference is actually in our attitudes toward whining. We accept crying as a normal part of baby and toddlerhood, but label the whining of a preschooler 'bratty' and 'spoiled' and refuse to listen to them until they 'use their normal voice' just when they need us to listen the most!

If we, as adults, would adjust our mindsets to accept the normalcy of whining, it would lose a bit of its power to annoy while enabling us to respond empathetically to our children when they're mustering all their newly-developed coping skills to avoid a meltdown.

So, what can we do when our little ones lapse into 'whine-eze' and we feel like tearing our hair out? Well, as always, an ounce of prevention is worth a pound of cure:

- Pay attention to the time of day whining seems to occur most often.

- Watch for triggers such as hunger, missed naps, and over-hurried schedules.

- Make whatever adjustments you can to prevent the whining before it starts.

- If all else fails and the whining does commence, remember that your little one is struggling to communicate in that moment. Respond by slowing down, sitting with them or kneeling down in front of them, and giving them your full attention.

- Use a quiet, soothing tone to reassure them, and listen patiently all the way through as they work their way back through the frustration and find the words to express themselves.

- You may not be able to give them the toy or snack or whatever else it is they want at that moment, but giving them the chance to be heard is often enough to forestall an all-out meltdown.

More than anything, though, giving your little ones the gift of your time and attention when they need it most (and often seem to deserve it least) will help foster that all-important connection that provides the basis for gentle guidance and boundary-setting. And, as an added bonus, children who feel heard tend to outgrow the whining stage much earlier than children who feel like they have to fight to be heard.

Chapter 14

Can We Talk?

Do you ever stop and really listen to the words coming out of your mouth and just cringe? I don't mean the common, everyday phrases like, *"The cat isn't a chew toy"* or *"Don't track the lava in the house"* or even *"Take the elephant out of your ear, please."*

Although the aforementioned might give us a moment of pause *(i.e. "Did I really just use those words in the same sentence?!?!")*, the words I'm referring to are those vague, unthinking, and downright confusing words we expect small people who are still at the beginning of the language learning curve, who are just figuring out how to articulate their own thoughts and feelings, and who are at our mercy if they don't respond to our satisfaction, to be able to process, understand, and obey.

Case in point:

Awhile back, my then-five-year-old was dawdling and fiddling with…well, pretty much everything as I was trying to get everyone into the van so we wouldn't be late for an appointment.

I said, *"Stop. Go."*

My little funnyface, being as precocious as she is witty, stopped stock-still, grinned, and raised her eyebrows, her eyes dancing in anticipation as she waited for me to hear it.

And then I did.

I smiled back and filled in the blanks, *"Please* stop *fiddling with things, and please* go *to the van."*

But what if I hadn't stopped to think? What if I had expected instant obedience? What if her still-limited grasp of all the ins and outs of human communication had prevented her from being able to quickly fill in the blanks I'd unintentionally left in my original directions?

In many authoritarian households, my sweet girl would have been the one to suffer for the adult's lack of clarity. With her limited ability to articulate her confusion, which would have been further inhibited if she'd been faced with a large, angry adult who may have been moving threateningly in her direction, she may well have been physically harmed in the name of 'discipline.'

Note: Discipline and punishment are not *the same, though they tend to be used interchangeably. Discipline is guidance toward desired behaviour, whereas punishment is a penalty for undesirable behaviour.*

And what of the other euphemisms and idioms and colloquialisms adults throw around like confetti on their own parenting parades?

What must a small child think when the person they love deeply and depend on absolutely says, *"You're killing me!"* or *"You're driving me up the wall!"* or *"I'm going to tear my hair out!"*

> *Mommy can die? I can make cars go up walls? Pulling hair hurts. Why would mommy hurt herself? Am I really that powerful? And dangerous? I must be really bad.*

How must they feel when faced with threats such as, *"I'm going to tear you up!"* and *"Don't make me spank you!"* and *"Stop crying or I'll give you something to cry about!"*

> *I can be torn up? Like trash? Am I trash? If I'm responsible for making you hit me, then are other people responsible if I hit them? I'm crying because I'm hurt and scared, that's not enough? I must not be worth much.*

The point is this: Language is powerful and complex. The words we use often have multiple meanings layered one on top of the other. And the words we don't use, the blanks we leave for others to fill in, carry many levels and possibilities of meaning.

Adults misunderstand one another on a regular basis, project their own experiences and perceptions into other's words, and make assumptions based on anything from an eyebrow twitch to a slight quirk of the lips.

How can we possibly expect little human beings who have just embarked on their journey in this new world with its nuanced language and often distracted and impatient adults to be able to instantly decode, process, and respond appropriately to our amorphous commands?

How much better, how much more effective, how much just flat-out kinder would it be if we were the ones to listen, to pay attention, to slow down and choose our words wisely, carefully, and compassionately?

Isn't communicating with these precious little sojourners in our homes for such a brief season of our lives worth the effort?

Chapter 15

Age of Reason:
Why, Oh Why, Do They Always Ask Why

Parenting can be difficult, no doubt about it. From inexplicable meltdowns to incessant whining to maddening tattling, the evolution of a child's communication skills can take a serious toll on a parent's patience. And just when a child's language skills become advanced enough for parents to begin to see the proverbial 'light at the end of the tunnel,' it hits… The 'Why' Zone.

"Why do birds have feathers and people have skin?"

"Why can't I have a rocket?"

"Why don't lakes have waves like the ocean does?"

"Why are oranges orange?"

"Why don't snakes have legs?"

"Why do people have to sleep?"

"Why don't monkeys wear clothes?"

"Why don't we live on the moon?"

"Why does ice have to be cold?"

"Why can't my frog sleep in my bed?"

"Why do we have hair?"

"Why can't I have cookies for breakfast…and lunch…and dinner?"

"Why don't clouds come in my window?"

Why? Why? Why do they always ask why? As annoying as it certainly can be, the 'why' stage serves several extremely important purposes.

It is during this stage that children have fully made the cognitive shift to understanding that they are an entirely separate person from their parents, and, in healthy parent/child relationships with that knowledge comes a need to 'investigate' their parents, find out what makes them tick, how they think, who they are. The ultimate purpose of this probing is identifying with their parents by examining and internalizing their values, knowledge, and belief systems.[5]

As children begin identifying with who their parents are, they are learning problem solving skills by listening to their parents' thought processes. They're also learning that their parents don't know everything, and they're learning that that's okay. Perhaps most importantly, they're learning that they can always go to their parents with questions, no matter how random or trivial they may seem at the time, a vital element in establishing and maintaining a strong communication channel for the later years of childhood and into adulthood.

And, really, would we want to eliminate the 'why's' even if we could? Asking 'why' is the sign of a healthy and natural curiosity. As Albert Einstein said, "The important thing is not to stop questioning. Curiosity has its own reason for existing."

Asking 'why' paves the way for discovery, invention, innovation, and creativity…

"*Why can't we fly?*" inspired Orville and Wilbur Wright to invent and fly the first fixed-wing airplane.

"*Why shouldn't we go into space?*" inspired Sergey Korolyov to design the first manned spacecraft.

"*Why shouldn't we be able to talk when we aren't together?*" inspired Alexander Graham Bell to invent the telephone.

"*Why shouldn't everyone have access to book?*" inspired Johannes Gutenberg to invent the moveable-type printing press.

"*Why don't we float off the earth?*" inspired Sir Isaac Newton to develop Newton's Law of Universal Gravitation.

"*Why doesn't gravity work exactly the same way on everything?*" inspired Albert Einstein to develop the Theory of Relativity.

So, while you're at your wit's end in the midst of The 'Why' Zone, keep reminding yourself of the important work your child is doing. Listen. Respond thoughtfully. Ask questions in return. Don't be afraid to say you don't know. That can be an excellent opportunity to head to the library for some interest-led learning.

Sharing yourself, your thoughts, your culture, and your values with your child; growing a strong, open communication channel; and encouraging a healthy curiosity are all invaluable investments in your child's future, even if they are at the expense of a bit of peace and quiet in the present!

Chapter 16

Five Gentle Tools for Handling Lying

The line between fantasy and reality is very blurry for small children. They still believe in Santa Claus and the Tooth Fairy. They are convinced that they can talk to animals and can fly if they wear a cape and are faster runners if they wear their 'fast shoes.' They think that the moon follows them home and that if they stretch as tall as they can, they can touch the stars. It's one of the most beautiful and celebrated facets of the innocence of childhood, but also one of the most misunderstood.

When a little boy puts a bowl on his head and makes up a fantastic story about rocketing to the moon in a cardboard spaceship, adults smile nostalgically and applaud his imagination. When that same little boy finds himself stuck in the uncomfortable position of being caught sneaking cookies from the pantry and makes up a story about the cookies accidentally falling off of the shelf into his mouth, those same adults often shame the child.

When a little girl perches on the arm of the sofa and tells a tall tale about pirates and stormy seas and walking the plank, her parents will laugh and join in the fun, but that same child will often be punished if she spins a tale to cover her tracks after she stuffs a towel down the toilet to see if it will flush and finds out that stuffed-up toilets overflow instead.

Communication is a complex skill, full of hidden nuances and subtle connotations and social mores that are far, far beyond the capacity of young children to understand. And yet they are often held to an impossible standard of perfection by the adults in their life.

Interestingly, those adults holding them to such a high standard rarely hold themselves to the same standard.

What adult, when faced with a traffic fine for speeding, hasn't protested that they didn't know they were going over the speed limit?

How often do adults say "I love your new haircut" or "You haven't aged a day" when the opposite is true?

How many adults call out of work sick when they aren't actually sick or return something to the store after using it and say it's unused or tell their spouse to say they aren't home when a phone call comes in they don't want to answer?

How, then, when adults are the ones modeling how communication should be used, can they expect children to somehow know instinctively when it is and isn't acceptable to lie? How can parents expect children to have the fortitude and maturity to simply accept the discomfort of telling the truth when they, themselves, so easily and so often lie to avoid their own discomfort?

And yet parents are often horrified and embarrassed when their child lies. So much so, in fact, that they react to their own emotions instead of responding appropriately to the child and the situation, and they end up shaming and/or punishing their child.

Think about it realistically for a moment, though. If children lie because they've seen the adults in their life lie, is shaming or punishing them fair? If they lie because they are uncomfortable and fearful, will making them more uncomfortable and fearful solve the problem? If they lie because it's normal for their developmental stage, does it seem reasonable to hold them accountable for it?

Having a few tools ready and available in your parenting 'toolbox' helps to avoid these ineffective and rather hypocritical adult reactions to children lying:

- First, be aware that the safer your children feel with you, the less likely they will be to lie. Removing the provocation of fear and discomfort will go a long way toward making your children trust you with the truth, no matter what it is.

- Second, even when children feel safe they may lie simply because small children often say how they wish things were and really believe they can make it happen just by saying it! Bearing this in mind can help you to see that innocent imagination at work that you enjoy so much in other settings and help you to exercise more patience and understanding.

- Third, when confronted with a lie, the best response is to calmly state the truth yourself, assure the child that they can always tell you the truth, and then move on without punishing the lie or giving the lie any more power or attention.

- Fourth, all behavior, including lying, is communication. Focusing on the need behind the behavior instead of the behavior itself or the lie it prompted will actually solve the problem rather than simply address the symptom of the problem.

- Fifth, keeping in mind that, over time, your children will mature enough to verbalize their needs instead of acting them out as long as their needs are met consistently and with understanding and respect while they are younger will help you to stay calm and focused. The end result will be healthy communication and trust with no need to lie.

Imagination truly is the language of childhood. It makes sense to try to understand their language instead of insisting they perfect ours. We are, after all, the only adults in the relationship.

Chapter 17

Rethinking Tattling

"She won't share!"

"He took my crayon!"

"They won't let me play with them!"

"He looked at me!"

"She poked me!"

"They're jumping on the couch!"

"He won't be my friend!"

Few things irritate adults as quickly as a tattle-tale. The kneejerk response is often *"Stop tattling!"* or *"Handle it yourself!"* or even to punish the little tattler.

But stop for a moment and think: What is being communicated? What is a child actually trying to tell us when they tattle? What message is a child getting by our response?

Tattling is, in effect, a child seeking wise counsel for a situation they don't know how to handle. When faced with a conflict that just weeks or months earlier would have resulted in tears or snatching or hitting or some combination of all three, a child who has matured and begun to develop some self-control is learning to stop and think instead of just react. But what do they do if no solution presents itself? What if they've tried to reason or negotiate with the object of their conflict and been unable to come to a resolution?

What do adults do when they don't know what to do? Typically, they either respond with maturity and seek out someone they respect and trust to help them deal with the situation, or they degenerate into chaotic emotions and resort to anger, power-plays, and manipulation. Often their response is influenced by their own childhood and how they were taught or not taught, as the case may be, to handle conflict.

When a child tattles, what they are actually doing is a rudimentary form of the advanced life skill of 'Pause. Think. Respond.' but they need help finding an appropriate and effective response. The child who seeks out an adult for guidance is indicating trust in the adult and respect for the adult's opinions and abilities. If the adult reacts with irritation, *"Stop tattling!"* or rejection, *"Handle it yourself!"* or punishment, the child learns not to trust, not to seek guidance, and not to share struggles and problems with those entrusted with their care, a potentially dangerous mentality, as we'll discuss later. In addition, an excellent teachable moment is lost.

When a child approaches a trusted adult with a problem, the child is saying, *"This is important. Hear me. Help me."* This is a wonderful opportunity to guide the child through the process of conflict resolution. So often we relegate life skills such as conflict resolution to textbooks and worksheets, if we address them at all. But learning is far more powerful and effective if it is tied to real-life, real-time issues that are important to us, that impact our lives, that matter.

So how do we handle the kneejerk irritation response when confronted with a tattling child? First, tossing out the tattling label entirely helps to adjust our mindset and focus on the child's need for guidance. We can rename it 'sharing' or whatever else will help us in the rethinking process (though in our home it is just a normal and accepted part of our parent/child interaction and doesn't have a name of its own to distinguish it from any other kind of communication).

Next, we can have prepared responses ready so that we aren't 'stuck' when we're trying to cope with our instinctive irritation in the same moment that we need to focus on helping an upset child in need of guidance.

Here are some possible responses:

If the child is over-wrought...

- *"I can see you're upset. Let's take a minute and breathe together, and then we'll be able to think clearly."*

When the child is calm enough to talk...

- *"Can you tell me what happened to upset you?"*

- *"Why do you think they did that?"*

- *"How do you think we should handle that?"*

- *"What could you have done differently?"*

- *"What would you want them to do if you had been the one to do that?"*

Often just feeling heard is enough to help the child find their own solution to the problem, but if further guidance is needed we can brainstorm solutions with them, walk them through some possible scenarios, or step in and help them to resolve the problem.

In addition to teaching valuable conflict resolution skills, giving our children the sure knowledge that they aren't alone in the world and don't have to cope with life on their own is a vital message. Logically speaking, does it really make sense to teach our children that they can't trust us with their problems, can't come to us when they're stressed and don't know how to cope, can't seek wise counsel when confronted with situations that are beyond their ability to handle?

The potential ramifications of that mindset are chilling. Can we really expect children to have the mental clarity and emotional maturity to be able to distinguish 'good' telling from 'bad' telling when faced with bullying or peer pressure or sexual predators? It's well known that sexual predators manipulate children with threats such as, *"No one will believe you,"* and, *"No one will listen, anyway."*

Guarding our children against those lies, against the bullies, against pressure from their peers is essential, and keeping the communication doors flung wide open is certainly a powerful step in the right direction.

Chapter 18

The Artist in the Child

The artistry and creativity of childhood extends far beyond stray crayon marks on walls, masterpieces hung on refrigerators, and colorful macaroni necklaces. Children are unique individuals with their own distinctive outlooks and perspectives. Each brings special gifts to the world that parents have the opportunity to nurture and inspire during the short season of childhood.

Watching our children blossom and become their own person is fascinating, but may be a bit disconcerting when their personalities and perspectives are significantly different from ours. Learning how to communicate with them effectively is the key to working with, instead of against, their uniqueness.

Sometimes that key to effective communication can be found in observing how our children observe the world. The artist in each child has a wonderfully unique perspective:

The Photographer is the child who captures the world in still shots, moments etched in their minds like photographs in an album, telling them who we are, who they are, what the world is like. This child defines the world in individual experiences, categorizing them, labeling them, and filing them away for future reference. Communicating with them is often most effective when centered around shared experiences, both good and bad. Conversations with The Photographer typically begin with, "Remember when...?"

The Painter is the child who sees the world in broad strokes, creating mental canvases of ever-changing hue and texture. This child often defines the world in ideals and possibilities rather than realities. Communicating with them tends to be most effective when phrased in language that supports their ideals while gently helping them to cope with reality. Conversations with The Painter often start with, "What if...?"

The Sculptor is the child who explores the world by chipping away at it, uncovering its dimensions and discovering its potential a layer at a time. This child defines the world in a series of challenges, digging and testing and pushing to find out the depth and breadth and possibility inherent in each moment, each person, each experience. Communicating with them is often most effective when their quest for knowledge is addressed first, before any attempt is made to redirect or correct. Conversations with The Sculptor tend to start with, "Why...?"

Embracing our children's perspective, taking the time to really know and appreciate them as individuals, communicating and connecting with them, and guiding them through childhood in an atmosphere of acceptance and unconditional love will free the artist in each of them to share their remarkable and unique beauty with the world.

Seeing the world through the lens of the artist in each of our children not only helps us to communicate and connect with them, but also gives us the gift of seeing the world through the eyes of a child again. And when our children have different personalities and perspectives from our own, as challenging as that can be as parents, seeing the world through their artistic lens may be an entirely new experience for us and broaden our understanding of the world in unexpected ways. Thus, the challenge becomes the gift, as is so often true in life.

Chapter 19

Whisper Words of Wisdom

"By words we learn thoughts, and by thoughts we learn life."
Jean Baptiste Girard

I love words. I love language. I love playing with old, staid quotes and classic literature titles, stories and legends, clichés and adages, and weaving them into unique or humorous settings.

But along with loving word play, I'm very aware of the power of language. Words can bring life, *"It's a boy!"* and love, *"I do!"* and words can bring death, *"I'm sorry. There's nothing more we can do."*

When it comes to raising children, the power of words cannot be overestimated. From how the labels we use influence our own perceptions of our children and their perceptions of themselves to how children's immature grasp of language limits their understanding and responses, words exercise immense power over the life of a child.

Just as important as being careful of the labels we use and having an understanding of language development in young children, though, or even more so, is being aware of the propensity for stressed and angry adults to 'power-up' on children and use language as a weapon. The lash of the tongue on the heart of a child can have devastating and lasting consequences.

"You stupid little idiot!"

"Can't you do anything right?"

"Why did I ever have you?"

"I hate my life!"

"You are totally useless!"

Words live and breathe and grow in our hearts until they either bear life-giving fruit ~ comfort, security, confidence…or fester into infectious, oozing wounds ~ despondency, anxiety, rage.

There is great truth to the belief that bullying begins at home. Children learn what they live. Just as violence begets violence, so angry parents tend to result in angry children, and parents who ridicule tend to produce sarcastic children, and critical parents tend to generate negative children.

Whether the children end up the bully or the bullied, aggressive with their peers or with themselves, cutting down others or cutting themselves, the fact is that hurting people hurt people, and children raised with condemnation in whatever form it takes are hurting people. Period.

Words matter. They matter desperately…as desperate as a five-year-old is to hear she's good, as desperate as a ten-year-old is to hear he's smart, as desperate as a fifteen-year-old is to hear she's valuable.

The truth is that we all make mistakes. We all say the wrong thing sometimes. We get angry and frustrated and overwhelmed and lash out at these tiny, impetuous, energetic, often incomprehensible, but always vulnerable little people we've been entrusted with the care and raising of. And often we don't apologize because we don't want to appear weak or to admit we've made a mistake or we'd rather just let it be or it doesn't even occur to us that we should apologize to a child. But words can heal, too, and an apology is a necessary step in the healing process.

But when verbal blows go untended, souls become scarred. When lashing out becomes the norm, damages begin to mount. And when children with battered souls grow into adults, the vicious cycle often continues in the form of domestic violence, substance abuse, or other destructive behaviors.

Parents, choose your words wisely, carefully, thoughtfully. In the same way that violence begets violence and anger begets anger, kindness begets kindness and peace begets peace. Sow words of peace, words that build, words that show respect and belief and support. Those are the seeds of a future filled with goodness and hope and compassion, and aren't those the things we really want for our children, after all?

Chapter 20

Love Means Sometimes Having to Say You're Sorry

It's been said that it takes ten positives to negate a negative, but the reality that most of us experience is that no amount of positives can fully erase a negative. While we may be able to forgive and move on, forgetting just isn't a possibility. Though we certainly do have the ability to control our reactions when confronted with criticism, taking what we can and learning and growing from it, the fact is that criticism marks us indelibly whether we like it or not.

We are human. Our hearts are tender and vulnerable, and we can be hurt. That is just a basic truth. And it is a truth that applies powerfully to the negative versus positive messages in our parenting and their relative impacts on our children.

I remember as a child being teased by my uncle for having big feet. He was actually referring to the fact that I was extremely tiny for my age, but I was too young to get the joke and didn't realize until I was an adult looking back on it how negatively it had affected me. The result was pain. Not just emotional pain, but actual physical pain because as a teen I consistently bought shoes that were too small because I was embarrassed about the size of my feet!

Despite the reassurances of my mother and friends, despite the fact that my feet were smaller than all of my friends' feet, in other words, despite all of the positive input and despite reality itself, I continued to be most strongly influenced by negative comments that were meant as affectionate jokes.

As parents, we will certainly have those moments when we say the wrong thing. We'll go to bed at night and cringe when we remember telling our preschooler that they're driving us crazy or our preteen that they talk too much or our teenager that they're impossible. We're human, too, and there's no getting around the fact that we can and will make mistakes.

What matters, what really, really matters, is what we do next. Our instinct may be to sweep the whole thing under the carpet and go on as if nothing happened (i.e. do an ostrich impersonation!). But what a powerful impact we can make if we value our children enough to take a deep breath and do that thing that no one likes to do, that thing parents often make children do whether they feel like it or not…what if we actually apologize to our children?

I promise, the world won't stop turning if we apologize to a child. In fact, the world will turn a little happier, at least in our little corner of it, if we live out how we want our children to turn out by owning up to our mistakes and taking responsibility for the hurt our words cause. In that moment of apology, not only will we model the positive life skill of taking ownership of our actions, but we will also bring healing and restoration to our relationship and, hopefully, prevent our children from carrying unnecessary baggage into their adulthood.

Remember, words can hurt, but they can heal, as well. We just have to be humane enough to overcome the ostrich-instinct!

Chapter 21

The sWord and the sTone

"What you do speaks so loud that I cannot hear what you say."
Ralph Waldo Emerson

We bring our precious little people into the world and pour our hearts and souls into lovingly raising…what?

How often do we stop and really think about what kind of a *person* we're trying to raise and what steps we're taking to accomplish that?

Character training seems to have gone out of style in some schools in favor of an all-out focus on standardized testing, but children need guidance and good examples of positive character traits if we want them to grow up to be productive members of our world. The good news is that parents who live out those positive character traits have a more powerful and lasting influence on children than any character training curriculum ever developed.

The first step, of course, is to decide just what character traits we want to model for our children. Here are a few examples of the kinds of traits we might want to focus on passing along to our children.

Generosity	*Compassion*	*Cheerfulness*
Honesty	*Friendliness*	*Self-control*
Helpfulness	*Creativity*	*Responsibility*
Resourcefulness	*Courage*	*Respect*

After considering what we want to model for our children, the next step is to look at how, or if, we're walking out those character traits in our life. Remember, our children will learn far, far more from watching what we do than from hearing what we say:

- We can lecture them eloquently about self-control, but if our children constantly see us angry and frustrated and yelling (i.e. lacking self-control), then that is what they'll internalize.

- We can preach daily sermons on honesty, but if our children see us lying to our supervisors (*'cough, cough'* *"Sorry, I can't come in to work today. I'm sick…See you later, kids, I'm going fishing!"*) and cheating on our taxes, that's what they will learn.

- We can rhapsodize about the value of compassion, but if our children see us ignoring their needs in favor of our own, judging instead of helping those in need, and gossiping about others' pain, that is how they will learn to live.

- We can pontificate about respecting our fellow human beings, but if we constantly show disrespect for our children's feelings by shaming them or ignoring their preferences and opinions; or disrespect for their belongings by using their possessions as tools to manipulate, threaten, and control them; or disrespect for their person by yanking, hitting, or manhandling them, then that is how they will learn to treat others.

The message here is this: *Consciously, intentionally, and consistently living out how we want our children to turn out is the most powerful and effective character training there is. The lessons they will take into the future will consist far more of how we treat them than what we teach them.*

Chapter 22

Chatterboxes and Dreamers:
Is Your Child an Introvert or an Extrovert?

From tantrums to whining to tattling to the endless 'why's,' the evolution of children's communication proceeds at a steady and relatively predictable pace, though the timing is influenced by factors such as individual personality, cognitive development, home environment, etc. Once children have a solid grasp of language and have developed more advanced reasoning and processing skills, and once they've examined the in's and out's of their parents' thoughts and beliefs, they begin to turn their attention to discovering their own interests and gifts and personalities.

Parents often begin to notice their children 'becoming their own person' during this time and we hear laments such as "She's eight going on eighteen" and "He's already changed career plans four times, and he's only ten!" It is during this period in childhood that children often develop into a chatterbox or a dreamer, though most will be unique combinations of the two.

When you have a chatterbox, whether you have a seven-year-old who could seemingly spend entire days describing every super hero's powers, weapons, weaknesses, enemies, and transportation or a nine-year-old who can list every horse breed, how to handle grooming, and what type of equipment to use for each kind of riding, the endless chattering can be deafening. The common theme is exploring who they are and what they like and what they think, all of which is accompanied by an intense need to share this fascinating process with the people they respect and admire the most…their parents, teachers, grandparents, siblings, anyone they've built a strong trust relationship with in their earlier years.

Chatterboxes can be challenging, to say the least. The never-ending talking, the intensity of their focus, and the often fickle nature of their passion (just when you get used to the daily commentary on the virtues of all things aquatic, their interest shifts and you're getting a lesson in martial arts that would make an encyclopedia look dumb!) can really keep you off-balance.

A common problem parents encounter at this stage is dealing with how to encourage their children in their interests without pushing them. So often when a child expresses interest in music their parent immediately buys a trumpet and enrolls him in lessons only to find that their budding Louis Armstrong has suddenly decided music is for the birds. His interests have flown elsewhere, and he's now too busy pursuing his new passion for veterinary medicine to bother with something so pedantic as practicing the trumpet!

While encouraging our children to follow through on their commitments is important, we need to let them lead the way as much as possible. One way to avoid this situation is to make sure that we aren't jumping into things too quickly rather than giving our children a chance to explore their interests unhindered by the demands and pressures of lessons and competitions.

The constant nature of the chatterbox's chattering can be grating on parental nerves, to be sure. However, not only allowing, but actually encouraging, our chatterboxes to share their thoughts as they begin to navigate the *"Who am I? What inspires me? What will I be?"* stage is important for a number of reasons:

- First, for a chatterbox, the need to be heard is intense, and it's a wise parent who meets that need. Not only does remaining open and available at this stage continue to build the trust that is so vital for a respectful and peaceful relationship, but it also sets the stage for healthy communication in the rapidly approaching teen years.

- Second, a child who is heard and encouraged in discovering themselves at this stage tends to enter adolescence a more well-grounded and focused individual. Young people who head into the teen years without having begun the process of self-discovery in middle childhood are more likely to be rudderless and vulnerable to peer pressure.

- Third, there is a unique window of clarity, a 'honeymoon' so to speak, in the middle years of childhood wherein language skills have been acquired, cognitive processes have matured, and the clouding of adolescent hormones and pressures and outside relationships aren't in the mix to muddy the waters. This is prime real estate for encouraging self-discovery while parental wisdom still seems wise to a child.

On the other end of the spectrum of middle childhood is the dreamer. Some children become extraordinarily introspective during this period. They are often lost in thought and may be perceived as inattentive or withdrawn. Oddly, it may seem harder to parent a dreamer because, while we rarely have to wonder what's going on in the mind of a chatterbox, it takes a constant, subtle level of awareness to stay in tune with a young dreamer. That awareness is vital, though, because your young dreamer still needs your attention and empathetic support and guidance, just in different ways.

Some of the subtleties to be aware of are:

- Signs of discomfort in social situations that they may not verbalize, but that we can offer insights into or alternatives to;

- Signs of anxiety such as frequent headaches or stomach aches which could be non-verbal cues that need our attention;

- Watching for what topics inspire their interest so we can encourage them on their road to self-discovery.

Checking in frequently with a dreamer is important since they may not volunteer information.

Asking questions such as *"That must have been difficult. Would you like to talk about it?"* and *"I feel like you're struggling with that. Can I help?"* along with observations such as *"You seem to find that interesting"* are discussion openers they may or may not take you up on, but let them know you care.

Don't push them to open up, though, by constant probing questions or being unwilling to follow their lead if they aren't ready to talk. Just create the opportunity for conversation and, if possible, do so at regular intervals and in a quiet place so that they know they can count on a private time to share when they are ready.

Prepare to simply sit in companionable silence during these times so your young dreamer won't feel rushed or pressured, but don't be surprised if they occasionally transform into a chatterbox and let all their pent up passions pour out at once before drifting back into their inner world.

Note: It is important to be aware of the subtle signs that can differentiate a dreamer from a withdrawn, angry, or depressed child. While a dreamer may often be in their own little world, it tends to be a happy world. If your child seems sad, is overly irritable, has trouble concentrating, seems unusually tired, becomes extremely sensitive to and negatively affected by social situations, etc. then it may be wise to seek a professional evaluation.

While the chatterbox and dreamer stage may be just that, a stage, and your child may grow out of the extroversion or introversion they appear to exhibit during this time, it's still helpful to examine the differences between those two personalities and find the best ways to communicate and interact with them.

Here is a helpful breakdown of the two ends of the extrovert/introvert spectrum that I shared in my last book *Two Thousand Kisses a Day: Gentle Parenting Through the Ages and Stages*:

Introverts:

- tend to think before they speak
- typically don't talk much
- are often uncomfortable in crowds
- tend to speak quietly and thoughtfully
- avoid the limelight
- tend to stick with an activity or conversation until it's finished
- often prefer written communication
- are often indecisive
- tend to be cautious
- tend to be shy or reserved
- often have one or two close friends
- tend to be focused, sometimes to the point of obsession
- are often serious
- tend to be thinkers

Extroverts:

- often like the limelight
- typically are comfortable in crowds
- often speak loudly and quickly
- tend to interrupt
- often have poor impulse control
- often jump from one activity to another
- tend to have trouble finishing tasks
- often think out loud
- tend to jump to conclusions
- are often decisive
- tend to be leaders
- are often easily distracted
- tend to be energetic and enthusiastic

- often are surrounded by friends
- tend to be doers

Once you have an idea what personality tendencies your child has, there are some key elements to consider when offering guidance and trying to communicate with them.

Introverts:

- often need a moment to think before responding to questions or requests
- need privacy when learning new skills
- respond more positively to guidance and praise when offered in private
- often need support when entering new situations
- tend to respond better to change when it is discussed in advance
- often need time to redirect their attention when absorbed in an activity
- don't respond well to being pushed into interacting with strangers
- often have a great need to have their personal space respected

Extroverts:

- tend to respond well when offered choices
- often need lots of physical affection and roughhousing
- respond better to independent exploration than guided teaching
- like to be complimented openly and publically
- need the freedom to try new things even when they haven't finished other things
- tend to work well in groups
- often still need time to redirect their attention when absorbed in an activity

These characteristics and suggestions aren't exhaustive, by any means, but they are springboards you can use to understand and communicate with your extroverts and introverts more intimately, effectively, and intentionally.

Chapter 23

I is for 'I dunno'
and That's Good Enough for Me

Remember the days when your little ones were just babbling their first ma-ma's and da-da's and Cookie Monster was the only adult conversation you heard all day? Remember feeling a bit at sea as you tried to figure out what each grunt and cry meant and how relieved you were when your tiny tot began using actual words to communicate, even if you had to really work to translate *"Mender tmowow I wost my dowie?"* into *"Remember yesterday when I lost my dolly?"*

Well, don't drop anchor in port just yet, parents of middles and teens, your days of feeling at sea aren't quite finished. Yes, their vocabulary may be nearly as large as yours and they may talk enough to drive you batty, but their ability to process, analyze, and articulate their emotions, especially the negative ones, is still far from mature.

Expecting them to be able to use words as easily and with as much insight as adults is like someone handing us a box of computer components and expecting us to be able to assemble, program, and operate the computer like an expert, but without the expert's knowledge and experience!

Our middles and teens still need help communicating their inner world to us, and that takes patience and understanding on our part while we give them time to process without adding the pressure of unrealistic expectations. Stress just increases their cortisol levels (cortisol is the stress-hormone associated with the 'fight-freeze-or-flight response' which essentially drains their brains of the ability to think just when they need to think the most!) which results in less communication, not more.

Case in point:

Recently, my Renaissance Girl injured her ankle while playing on the back porch with our new kittens. (Yes, you read that right, first of my six to end up in the ER from playing with kittens!) She's newly thirteen, and the hospital staff all directed their questions to her instead of to me. I stood back quietly and let her navigate this new ground as long as she was comfortable, but when she started shooting me panicked glances, I stepped in and helped her out.

One of the doctors rather abrasively said that she should be able to answer all of the questions herself, and I literally watched her shut down. The next question was her birthday, and she couldn't remember it. She was already in pain and embarrassed (mainly because self-consciousness and the resulting embarrassment is just a fact of life at thirteen, poor thing) and the doctor putting pressure on her like that just sent her stress level soaring. I redirected his attention to me and handled the rest of the interview myself.

When the doctor left, I quietly waited to give my girl time to process. After a few moments, she said, *"All those eyes looking at me...I couldn't think!"* We chatted for a moment about it, and I told her about my absolute refusal to walk up to the counter at McDonald's and ask for a ketchup package one day when I was her age. I remember not being able to explain why it made me so uncomfortable, but looking back it was probably a combination of worrying about people ignoring me while I stood there (as happens all the time to middles and teens, unfortunately), and suddenly remembering I hadn't shaved my legs that morning, and feeling like my shirt was unflattering, and a dozen other thoughts that raced through my head, but I couldn't articulate at the time with anything more than a shrug.

So when you ask how your middle or teen's day went at school and get that classic shrug, or when you notice they're a bit down and ask what's wrong and get an *"I dunno,"* remember, they aren't really giving you the brush off, they just aren't ready or able to put their day or feelings into words. Pressing them to talk before they're ready only increases their stress, which in turn causes that mind-numbing cortisol to flood their brains and slows down their processing abilities even more.

I've found that it's far better to let them know I'm available to talk when they are and then let it go until later. When the house is quiet for the night and everyone else is asleep, my middles and teens tend to open up like night-blooming flowers. If I know they need to talk, I'll tap on their door and wait until I'm invited in, then sit on their bed and start chatting lightly about the day. After a bit, we'll lapse into a comfortable silence, and then, sure enough, the words start coming. Sometimes they come out all in a tumble, sometimes slowly, awkwardly, but they get it out there so we can take a look at things and process them together.

Sometimes, though, I'm the one who hears a little tap on my door and a head poking through to see if I'm awake. We do some fancy hand signals while they let me know they need to talk and I let them know if the baby's still nursing to sleep and they need to wait a few minutes or if I can slip away and join them immediately.

In an odd way, this time of their lives feels like a return to the nighttime neediness of infancy. One of the payoffs to the gentleness and consistency in meeting their nighttime needs then is their assurance that their needs will be met now. They seem to be more likely to approach me with the need for one of our 'midnight talks' based on the confidence that I'm available to them, day or night, rather than being hesitant because they are unsure of their reception.

The heart of the matter, though, isn't what time these chats take place. It's that they take place when our middles and teens are ready to share, when they've had time to process their experiences enough to get them out in the open where we can work through the rest of whatever processing, analyzing or interpreting they need.

Through these interactions with our children we are not only helping them to get things out instead of bottling them up, but we are also letting them know in a very tangible and practical way that they are not alone in coping with life, a valuable lesson indeed when you consider that one of the mantras of depressed, bullied, and/or suicidal youth is *"I feel so alone."*

In addition, rather than being an indication of immaturity or undesirable dependency, a child being willing to talk through the challenges and ordinary stresses of life is actually showing a healthy openness to sharing and growing. And the beauty of it is that each time we help our children through the 'processing process,' it prepares them to do a bit more themselves the next time, and the next, and the next until one day we realize we haven't heard that little midnight tap on our door in a while, and we sleep a bit better in the knowledge of a job well done.

Chapter 24

Backtalk is Communication...LISTEN

With more than 90% of parents admitting to spanking or otherwise physically punishing their children at least occasionally, mainstream American parenting can certainly be defined as punitive. If you go to the library or browse the shelves at Barnes & Noble or check out Amazon's best sellers in the parenting genre, you will find a predominance of popular, punishment-based, obedience-focused parenting guides. Whether its spanking or time outs or removal of privileges or time confined in their room, the vast majority of children in the United States are raised with punitive parenting.

When it comes to children talking back to parents, many of these punitive parenting guides dictate a zero-tolerance policy. By their definition, backtalk is often characterized as verbal or emotional abuse of parents, defiance, rudeness, or threats:

- Verbal or emotional abuse of parents is considered any statement that insults or hurts a parent such as, *"You're so mean!"* or *"I wish I didn't even have parents!"* or *"I hate you!"*

- Defiance is any statement containing the word *"No"* in response to a parental command.

- Rudeness is defined as anything from deep sighs to rolled eyes to stomped feet.

- Threats are any statements that give conditions such as, *"If you take away my cell phone, I'll just go get a new one!"* or *"If you don't drive me to my friend's house, I'm walking there!"*

These parenting guides direct parents to decide which punishment to mete out when their child talks back to them, specifying that the deciding factor should be whichever punishment would be the most unpleasant, painful, and distressing for the child. Punishments are to be carried out swiftly and without discussion. When the retribution for the child's actions is over, it is to be followed with a lecture laying down the laws of the family. Again, no discussion is allowed, but if the child expresses appropriate penitence, love and hugs can then be offered.

In addition to the sick feeling in the pit of my stomach at the thought of children being subjected to this kind of harsh, punitive parenting, I'm saddened by the upside-down reasoning that shuts communication down instead of utilizing it to bring healing, understanding, and restoration to the parent/child relationship.

Take a look at the order of parenting prescribed: First, *punishment* meted out by the parent. Second, *lecture* delivered by the parent. Third, *conditional reconnection* based on a proper expression of remorse to the parent from the child.

In gentle parenting, the order and intent of parenting would be the polar opposite: First would come *listening* for the need behind the behavior and reconnecting with the child at the point of need. Second, would be initiating a two-way *communication* about the problem and brainstorming about how to address the issue in ways that will meet everyone's needs. Third, would be offering *guidance* and equipping the child with better ways to express needs in the future.

The punitive parenting approach focuses on the child *as* the problem and attempts to solve the problem by 'fixing' the child through intentionally unpleasant external forces.

The gentle parenting approach focuses on the child *having* a problem and attempts to help the child solve the problem through connection, communication, and inviting cooperation.

Now look at the definitions of backtalk--verbal and emotional abuse of parents, defiance, rudeness, and threats. The questions that immediately arise are: What about the parents? Are they held to the same standards as the children? Or do they threaten? Do they say 'No'? Do they sigh? Do they hurt their children?

As parents, our actions will always be reflected in our children's behavior. Children learn what they live. No amount of lecturing can undo the powerful impact on a child of their parent's own behavior and choices.

When a child backtalks, sometimes also referred to as mouthing-off or sassing, they are in the throes of a huge, internal maelstrom of emotion. Whatever they are reacting to in the moment, whether it's being told 'no' about something or being asked to do or not do something, it is rarely those issues that are at the root of the problem. The moment at hand is just the tipping point causing a fissure in the child's heart that lets out a bit of the steam inside. The real concern should be that there is, metaphorically, steam in the child's heart to begin with.

It is at this point that parents have the opportunity to model self-control and self-regulation by controlling their own knee-jerk reaction to their child's backtalk. Instead of meeting fire with fire, childish outburst with childish parental outburst, child's tantrum with adult tantrum, parents can slow down, breathe through their own emotions, and then listen through the fiery storm of their child's words to the hurt, fear, and anger behind the words.

In the same way that "a gentle answer turns away wrath,"[6] a soft-voiced, *"Let's take a minute and calm down so we can work through this together, okay?"* from a parent is a magical, healing balm that immediately begins to diffuse tough situations and creates an atmosphere in which connection and communication can bring effective, peaceful solutions not only to the issue at hand, but to the inner turmoil that prompted the outburst in the first place.

Meeting a child at their point of need when that need is expressed through meltdowns, yelling, disrespect, or defiance takes patience, self-control, and empathy on the part of a parent, which can be a huge growth experience for the parent if they, themselves, were not parented that way. But the impact of living those positive life skills in front of our children is immeasurable.

Parenting isn't a perfect science and parents aren't perfect people, but creating an overall atmosphere of respect in a home starts with the parents modeling respect in their own tone of voice, in their own reactions to stressful situations, in their own interactions with their children.

It's not easy, for sure. But the best things, the most valuable things, in life rarely are. Working toward being understanding, available, and responsive to our children's needs yields a priceless return in our relationship as the years fly by and adulthood looms. Not meeting those needs, though, may have serious negative consequences...

Dear Daughter,

You entered your teen years with a bang a few years ago, and the explosions have been shattering our home ever since. I've begged, threatened, bribed, and punished; cried, shouted, and bargained; but I just can't find a way to reach you anymore. You constantly say I don't listen to you, but how can I when you won't talk to me? You say I don't understand you, but how can I when you push me away? You say we aren't a family, but then spend every day with earphones in your ears, blocking us out. You ask me why I hate you, then roll your eyes when I tell you I love you. How did it come to this? We used to be such a happy family. Please, let me be there for you during this huge transition in your life. Let's really try to communicate with each other. I'm just lost here, honey, and I need you to reach out and help me reconnect with you. I love you.

Your Dad

'Dear' Dad,

Happy family? Are you kidding me? No, I guess not.
You never did get it. Okay, you asked, so I'll tell you.
You were always happy because you were always in
control. Want to know why I don't talk to you now?
Because you never listened when I was little. When I
was scared in my room at night and called you, you
either ignored me or threatened to spank me if I didn't
go to sleep. I'd lay there, crying so hard I'd almost
throw up, terrified of the sounds and shadows in my
room, but even more terrified of you. So, sorry, but I
don't buy that you're 'there for me' when it's only ever
been at your own convenience. When you were mad at
something I'd done and I tried to explain myself, you'd
call it backtalk and smack me in the mouth. So forgive
me if I don't really believe you when you say you want
to 'communicate' with me now. When I'd try to show
you a dance I'd made up or tell you about how
someone had pushed me on the playground, you
couldn't even be bothered to look away from your
stupid computer while I was talking, so if I'm wrapped
up in my electronics, I learned that little trick from you,
Father Dear. Oh, and reconnect? Really? That implies
that we were once connected. But when I was a little
girl and invited you into my world and asked you to
play with me, you were always too busy. So if you don't
understand me, sorry, but that invitation expired years
ago. Want to know why I think you hate me? Because
your actions told me so. Your 'love' is just words.

'Your' Daughter

Not all children react this way to harsh, punitive, control-based parenting, of course. Some children, due to personality, other influences and mentors in their lives, or simply as a survival instinct, will turn out okay despite how they are parented.

But 'okay' is too mediocre a goal when it comes to growing our children into the adults who will one day lead our world. Instead of raising children who turn out okay *despite* their childhood, let's raise children who turn out extraordinary *because of* their childhood. Let's grow excellent, outstanding, remarkable adults who will be world changers for the next generation and the generations to come.

Chapter 25

My Huckleberry Friend

For the same reasons that I tell my children that police officers are our friends, I want my children to view me as their friend. I don't just want to be my children's buddy or pal or playmate. I want to be their very best, true-blue, got-your-back, no-holds-barred friend.

Sometimes we get so caught up in preparing our children for the future we forget that one of the things that will define their future is their relationship with us in the present. If our relationship is characterized by constant commands, demands, criticisms, and corrections, our children's trust in us and their conception of authority in general may become skewed.

When they become adults, then, instead of viewing authority figures such as bosses, supervisors, and police officers as friends and allies, and instead of having the innate desire to cooperate with them, our children are more likely to view them with suspicion and distrust and try to avoid them or 'get things past them' rather than to comfortably work with them.

Think about these definitions of a friend in the context of parenting:

"A friend is one that knows you as you are, understands where you have been, accepts what you have become, and still, gently allows you to grow." William Shakespeare

"Friendship is the inexpressible comfort of feeling safe with a person, having neither to weigh thoughts nor measure words." George Eliot

"It is not so much our friends' help that helps us as the confident knowledge that they will help us." Epicurus

"My best friend is the one who brings out the best in me." Henry Ford

"As a friend, you first give your understanding, then you try to understand." Robert Brault

And definitions from an informal friendship poll…

- A friend is a person who smiles when they see you, every time, because they really like you.

- A friend listens when you speak and speaks when they know you're ready to listen.

- Friends are people who challenge you, but never condemn you.

- True friends stick by you even when whatever you're dealing with isn't their problem and doesn't affect them personally.

- A friend is always honest, even when being honest is hard.

- A real friend knows when not to talk, just be there.

- A real friend answers your phone call, every time, any time, day or night, no matter what.

- True friends are real about their own struggles. They don't act like they're perfect. And that's why you can be real with them and not have to act like you're perfect, either.

- A friend is someone you love to spend time with, someone you really enjoy and who enjoys you back.

- A friend is someone who has time for your pain even when you're kind of being a pain about it.

- A good friend is kind and shares and you can totally relax with them.

- Friends are people who you can be silly and goofy and dorky with one minute and who will hold you if you need to cry the next minute, and they don't even have to know why.

- A friend is someone who is always friendly and smiles a lot.

- Friends are people who like you just the way you are, but still help you to be better.

- A friend listens with empathy when you've messed up, speaks the truth in love, and offers to help you fix what needs to be fixed, no matter what it takes.

- A real friend isn't afraid to say hard things to you because they've already proven that they love you.

- True friends don't expect you to change to suit them. They accept you, period. But they'll do whatever it takes to help you change what you want to change.

- A friend is a friend all the time, even when you're not very likeable.

- A true friend trusts you, even when you make mistakes, even when you fail them, even when you show up late to everything, they still trust you.

- A friend loves you at ALL times, and they show it.

- Friendship is about accepting someone for who they are and not always having to agree with them, but loving them enough to tell them if they're headed in the wrong direction.

- A friend is someone you respect and who respects you.

- Friendship isn't about always being right, it's about always being right with our friends.

- A true friend always gives you the benefit of the doubt.

- Friends are ready, willing, and able to believe the best about you instead of assuming the worst.

- A friend is someone you can trust.

- A real friend is never afraid to come to you, and you're never afraid to go to them, ever.

- A friend is someone who'll give you the cookie that wasn't dropped on the floor, even if you wouldn't know the difference.

- A true friend is someone you can trust not to say something about you when you aren't with them that they wouldn't say when you are.

- Friends are fair, but they're not fair-weather friends, they're always there.

- True friends understand you even when you don't understand yourself. They can do that because they've taken the time to get to know you through and through.

- Real friends listen to your heart, not just your words.

- A friend is always kind even when you don't deserve kindness.

- A friend is never inconvenienced by you. Friendship isn't about convenience, it's about unconditional love, sacrifice, loyalty, and laughter.

- Friends listen first and speak later.

- A friend still sees your beauty even when the ugly in you is showing.

As a parent these definitions of friendship capture eloquently the gifts I want to give my children: the gift of guidance, the gift of support, the gift of grace, the gift of kindness, the gift of understanding, the gift of loyalty, the gift of trust, the gift of respect, the gift of generosity, the gift of acceptance, and so much more.

Sharing these gifts with our children is like planting a garden with the seeds of the characteristics we want to pass along to them, then watering those seeds with the gentle rain of our unconditional love. What blossoms in their hearts and lives is exactly what we plant, producing a harvest of kindness, goodness, generosity of spirit, respect for others, and grace for themselves and the world around them.

Chapter 26

Whispering Winds of Change

It's no secret that many parents dread the teen years as much as, if not more than, they do the toddler years. With society's propensity for blaming social issues on 'kids these days,' and struggling, frustrated parents seeking support by sharing stories of their teens' attitudes and ingratitudes, it's not surprising that adolescence gets a bad rap.

But the truth is that teens are just people like the rest of us, subject to human imperfections and simply trying to find their place in the world. They may have some hormonal ups and downs, but just as women don't appreciate being grouped together and defined by exaggerated stories of PMS and men don't like every decision they make in middle-age to be labeled evidence of a midlife crisis, teens don't deserve that kind of disrespectful stereotyping either.

The thing is, adolescent behaviors that parents fear most such as rebellion, drug use, eating disorders, etc. don't just appear out of nowhere. Teens don't grow up in a vacuum. Our early parenting choices matter. We are, literally, building our relationship with our teens while we're parenting our toddlers and preschoolers.

Ideally, preparation for the teen years begins in infancy as we spend those first months of our child's life laying a foundation of trust. Then in the toddler years that preparation continues as we establish safe and reasonable boundaries with gentle guidance, patience, and proactive parenting like planning shopping trips around naps and bringing along snacks and toys to avoid tantrum triggers.

In the preschool and middle years, preparation for adolescence builds on the trust foundation we laid in the first months and years of our teen's life as we grow a spirit of cooperation rather than compulsory compliance, establish a healthy relationship with our child based on teamwork instead of a dictatorship based on forced obedience, and create strong lines of communication rooted in hearing and being heard rather than the often-closed hearts and minds that result from lecture-based parenting.

The result…

- Children who don't have to fight for independence because they don't have anything to rebel against or any motivation for rebellion.

- Children who feel that they are respected and that their opinions are heard and valued and therefore don't have the angst to fuel negative attitudes.

- Children who trust and feel trusted and don't want to lose what they instinctively know is of great value ~ our mutual trust relationship.

Thus the groundwork is set for gently parenting through the teen years.

Once we've done the groundwork for the teen years, preparation shifts from preparing for adolescence to preparing our adolescents for adulthood. In the day-to-day parenting of teens, preparation means getting them and ourselves ready for their advent into adulthood by intentionally and incrementally handing over the reins of their lives into their inexperienced, but capable hands.

Another aspect of parenting our teens is participation. In the early years, participation means joining our little ones as they explore the world with mud-splattered walks in the rain and building tilted block towers which tumble and are rebuilt time and again. It means reading bedtime stories and welcoming midnight visitors in our beds and sharing morning tickle-fests and kissing imaginary boo-boos.

In the teen years participation means much the same, only instead of blocks tumbling, it's plans and hopes and hearts that sometimes tumble into disappointments and need our support and understanding to be rebuilt. It's midnight visitors who tap softly on our door and ask if we can chat for a bit. It's shared hugs and cheers and tears and whispers of encouragement. It's being there, being aware, being in-tune. It's active, proactive, and intentional parenting.

And, finally, how we interpret our children's behavior in the early years sets the stage in a very real way for how we interpret their behavior in adolescence. In the early years, interpretation means that instead of assigning negative ulterior motives to our little ones' crying, curiosity, outbursts, explorations, tantrums, and other behaviors, we seek to interpret what they are communicating and empathize with and validate their emotions. It means we try to meet the needs behind the behaviors first, opening the door to gentle guidance so that we can equip them with better ways of expressing their needs as they grow and mature.

Interpretation in the teen years means exactly the same. We listen, assume the best, meet needs, listen more, give grace for being human, empathize with and validate emotions, listen and listen some more, and continue to create open hearts and minds through connection and communication so that our gentle guidance can be heard and received and trusted.

If you are new to gentle parenting and need help rebuilding and healing your relationship with your teen, check out Appendix A in the back of the book for some ideas that may help.

Chapter 27

Messages in a Bottle:
Our Hope for the Future

"Children are the living messages we send to a time
we will not see."
Neil Postman

From the time our children enter the world, fresh and new like the snowy pages of an unwritten journal, and on through their toddlerhood, preschool years, middle childhood, and beyond, communication is the instrument with which we compose our relationship. Listening, responding, understanding, guiding, and interacting are all inscribed as the messages we communicate both verbally and non-verbally.

It is those messages that we communicate back and forth, back and forth in the everyday ebb and flow of life that weave the threads of relationship, create the bonds of family, and ultimately become the inner guidebook our children will live by throughout their lives. They are the messages in a bottle that we will send into the future to speak our hearts, our beliefs, our hopes, our values, our support, and our love to our children when we can no longer be with them. In a very real way, we are writing our own future, the future of our world, on the hearts and minds of our children.

It makes sense, then, to be intentional about the messages we share, to think long and hard about how our choices and actions will impact tomorrow's world leaders, to choose our words wisely and carefully so that they don't scar the hearts that carry the lifeblood of the future.

Here are some of the messages I am intentionally writing into my children's future:

- You are capable, but never be ashamed to ask for help when you need it.

- You are good, but you're not perfect.

- You will make mistakes, and that's okay.

- Celebrate the gifts you've been given and use them wisely, but don't forget that others have gifts of great value, as well.

- Take the time to recognize and appreciate other people's gifts or you'll miss wonderful opportunities to learn and grow.

- You are strong, but you don't always have to be.

- It's okay to take a break from being strong and rest in someone else's strength when you need to. That's why you have family and friends.

- You will make it through whatever life throws at you, but often making it through won't look like you thought it would.

- For every strength, there is a weakness.

- Build on your strengths, and guard against your weaknesses. Awareness is half the battle.

- Not everyone will agree with your life-view, and that's okay.

- It's not your job to make others live their lives by your standards.

- It is your job to live your life by your standards.

- Success has nothing to do with money.

- Success has everything to do with people.

- The most successful people are not the ones who get the most; they're the ones who give the most.

- The best leaders are those who lead by example and who aren't afraid to strap on a pair of boots and break a sweat.

- Respect must be earned, by you and others. Never give it away freely, and never expect it without working for it.

- Kindness is always the right answer.

- The more happiness you share, the happier you'll be.

- Love isn't a feeling; it's a choice.

- Choose love, always. That means choosing patience, kindness, forgiveness, humility, hope, and trust.

- Problems are just opportunities to find new solutions.

- Failure has its own rewards. Learn from your failures and move on.

- Hurt is a part of life. People will hurt you. Life will hurt you. It's okay to be angry.

- Anger is a normal human emotion. Hate is not. Work through anger toward forgiveness or it will end in hate, and you'll be the one in bondage.

- You are in charge of your life. You decide what you will do, what you will not do, who you will love, who you won't love, who will be in your life, who won't be in your life, who you will be, who you will not be. Choose wisely.

- There is always hope. Never forget that.

- If you look for the good in people, you will find it.

- Life is beautiful, but sometimes you have to look for the beauty in the ashes.

- Laughter is beautiful. Laugh every day, on purpose.

- Dream. Set goals. Make things happen. Life is what you make it.

It is these messages and others that we send with our children as they leave our homes and become the next world leaders, teachers, artists, writers, comedians, grocery clerks, therapists, mechanics, doctors, researchers, thinkers, dreamers, midwives, preachers, mothers, fathers, inventors, painters, cab drivers, and humanitarians that will create the future of our world. Let's think deeply, love selflessly, and act intentionally to write messages of peace and goodness and generosity of spirit on the hearts and minds of our children, our messengers, our hope for a better tomorrow.

Tips for Talking to Teens

*From *Two Thousand Kisses a Day: Gentle Parenting Through the Ages and Stages*

Communication is always a huge concern for parents of adolescents. The strong, open communication channel created and mutual respect and trust foundation established in the early years through gentle parenting provide a powerful platform for a healthy parent/teen relationship. Simply put, children and teens who feel heard and understood and respected don't need to fight to be heard, understood, and respected. Or, conversely, they don't slip away into the sullen, angry, withdrawn teen who doesn't bother to even try to be heard anymore because they never felt heard or understood as a young child.

Again, this is not to say that the gently raised adolescent will be perfect. None of us are! But with a healthy relationship based on open, honest communication, issues can be addressed as they arise and in a respectful and timely manner instead of a teen feeling the need to go 'underground' with their behavior or problems.

So, that said, what are some practical tips for talking to teens?

1. *Honesty is paramount.* Teens will tune out faster than you can imagine if they sense you're being less than transparent with them. Only in a mutually honest environment will a teen be willing to share their deepest fears, hopes, disappointments, etc.

2. *Judgment-free zone.* Along with this goes the need to be able to say anything, anything at all, and know that they will be heard and accepted without judgment, without repercussion. Consequences for broken rules should never come as a result of a heart-to-heart discussion, or it may well be the last heart-to-heart your teen will have with you. You can and should honestly express your concern and even disappointment if appropriate, but don't make it all about yourself or the conversation and chance for real connection will end.

3. *Respect is key.* Embarrassment is like Kryptonite to a teen. Ridiculing them, making light of their feelings, minimizing their experiences by 'one-upping' them with yours are surefire ways to shut down a conversation with a teen permanently.

4. *Reassurance is healing.* Teens need to know they are normal. They need to hear that everyone has 'bad' thoughts sometimes and that doesn't make them 'bad person.' Sharing some crazy thoughts that have popped into your head through the years and how "It's not the thought, it's what you do with the thought that matters" will help them realize they aren't abnormal. (You'd be surprised how many teens think they're abnormal! 'Normal' matters to them HUGELY.)

5. *Burn the midnight oil.* Adolescents seem to be naturally nocturnal creatures. When the house is quiet and nothing is competing for attention, guards begin to drop, emotions mellow, and in the stillness of the night, soft-voiced conversations invite deep, meaningful discussions. Don't let the busyness and business of life rob you of these sweet moments with your teens who will so very soon be off on their own in the adult world.

Dealing with the Hard Stuff

Addressing difficult life issues with teens is not something most parents look forward to, particularly, and often flat out dread. Some parents just don't address these issues, period, often with excuses such as, *"They need to find out what they believe for themselves."*

But simply avoiding talking about difficult issues doesn't make them go away, and often teens left to fend for themselves become overwhelmed with societal pressures, an endless array of choices, and conflicting information. Leaving them to *"figure out what they believe themselves"* just leaves them without the guidance and wisdom they need from those they trust the most and may lead to feelings of resentment and abandonment as well as poor choices.

It can, of course, be challenging to address hard issues like sex, morality, war, politics, religion, etc. with your teen. Teenagers do a fantastic imitation of bloodhounds. Hypocrisy, fear, 'smudging' the truth, you name it, they can sniff it out in a heartbeat! When talking about these difficult life issues, it's far better to be transparent about any doubts or failings or confusion you may have because your teen will know if you try to gloss it over.

Got some skeletons in your closet? Dust them off and pull them out as object lessons and connection points. Your teen will learn more from one confession (no need to go into graphic detail) than from a hundred lectures.

Ambivalent about current events? Discuss the inner conflict you're having.

Passionate about your spiritual beliefs? Tell them how that feels and what brought you to that point.

Sharing your heart, your experiences, your struggles, honestly and often, with your teen will make an impact on them that no amount of bookwork or lecturing or training can possibly match. Keep in mind, too, that this is a life conversation and not just confined to adolescence. Beginning this kind of sharing early in your child's life in age-appropriate ways establishes the vital communication channel that is central to gentle parenting, and keeping the conversation open-ended helps to maintain healthy familial ties with your children even when they're adults, themselves. Remember, we never outgrow the human need for connection!

Too Late for Teens?

So what do you do if you're the parent of a teenager and have only just discovered gentle parenting? Is it too late to implement any of the gentle parenting philosophy to establish connectedness and mutual respect and ease the transition into adulthood? And what if your teenager is in full-on rebellion mode? Is there anything gentle parenting can do for you?

The answers aren't easy, by any means. Making changes at this stage is as challenging as teens themselves can be. But, that said, there are some basic tenets that you can begin the hard work of weaving into your parenting even at this late stage:

1. *Don't engage.* Win or lose, they'll enjoy the argument, and you won't. As my grandmother always used to say, "Never wrestle with a pig. They'll love the roll in the mud whether they win or lose, and you'll just get muddy." Translated, that means that teens often simply enjoy a good debate, while adults just get frustrated.

2. *Apologize.* Take responsibility for past and present parenting mistakes. As mentioned earlier, teens can sniff out hypocrisy like bloodhounds, and acting like you're perfect (which is how they'll interpret that missing apology) smells an awful lot like hypocrisy to them.

3. *Be real.* Nothing will make a teen more resentful than you demanding behavior from them that you aren't modeling in your own life.

4. *Be available.* If you haven't been available in the past, openly let your teen know that you've made mistakes and would like to change, then let them know you are available to them, day or night, whether your favorite tv show is on or not, even if you have work to do, or emails to read, or phone calls to return…no matter what. Don't be surprised if they test you on this. Even adults tend to test out changes before we fully believe we can count on them!

5. *Communicate.* If you feel your early parenting hasn't established the open communication vital to a healthy parent/teen relationship, it isn't too late to make some renovations to bridge the gap. Just start talking…about your own life, your own struggles, your own needs, and just start sharing, about your love for them, your hopes for them, your pride in them. And start asking questions, not prying, but providing an opening for them to talk about their lives. If they aren't ready to open up yet, don't push. Just be there, ready to listen when they're ready to talk.

6. *Let go.* When a child reaches the teen years, it's time to begin slowly releasing them from parental controls and start letting them make more of their own choices. This is not to say that you stop being their parent, but that you begin to consciously shift your role in your teen's life further and further away from guardian and caretaker, and closer and closer to a supportive, accepting, mentoring role…in short, a friendship role that will set the stage for your relationship with your adult child. This conscious shifting on your part will help to make your teen's transition from child to adult a cooperative effort between you rather than a source of conflict.

7. *Move.* If your teen is involved with a bad group, is immersed in drugs, gangs, etc…pack up and move. I know it's easier said than done. I know there are all kinds of job and economic issues involved. I know it's a huge sacrifice. And I know they'll fight you on it. But if everything else has failed, removing them from negative influences and situations to give them a chance at a fresh start may be the best, or only, choice. And, letting your teen know that they are the first and most important priority in your life, more important than your job, home, the life you've built, or anything else, will in and of itself go a long way toward healing your relationship. *Note: Blaming your teen for the move, inwardly or outwardly, will undermine your reasons for moving. Make peace in your own heart with the move ahead of time so you'll be up to the challenges inherent in all big life changes.

Appendix B

Twelve Steps to Gentle Parenting:
Setting Yourself Up for Success

*From Two Thousand Kisses a Day: Gentle Parenting Through
the Ages and Stages*

It's been said that it takes twenty-one days to make or break a
habit and that change comes easiest and lasts longest when it's
undertaken in small, bite-sized chunks. Those same principles
apply when trying to transform your parenting, as well. Simply
resolving on January 1st that, from that day forward, you are
going to be a gentle parent and trying to change everything all at
once is just setting yourself up for disappointment, frustration,
and, more than likely, failure, followed by that age-old enemy of
peace…mommy guilt.

Instead, try setting yourself up for success by taking a year of
'baby steps' to create real, lasting transformation in your
parenting. Here are twelve steps you can start any time of the
year, not just on January 1st, that offer practical, effective
guidance to help you on your journey to gentle parenting. Keep
in mind, though, that failure is a natural, normal part of change,
so remember to give yourself grace when you fail. (Also, giving
yourself grace is good practice for learning to extend that same
grace to your children, which is a hallmark of gentle parenting!)

January (Step 1)

Slow down! ~ Gentle parenting is, at its core, based on a strong,
healthy parent/child connection, so intentionally including time
in your life to build and maintain that connection is vital. Start

the year off by examining your daily and weekly schedule and looking for things to reduce or eliminate. Add up how much time your children spend in school, sleeping, in daycare, with babysitters, at sports practices, in music lessons, etc. and look at how much or little time is left over. Time for your family to connect, time to play, time to simply be, are just as important as those other activities, if not more so! Eliminate and reduce what you can, and look for ways to build connection into the things you can't eliminate. For instance, if your child has homework each night, why not sit down and work through the homework with them? As humans, we learn better through interaction, anyway, so you'll not only be connecting, you'll be enriching your child's education in the process! Another area that might benefit from a connection 'rehab' is that morning rush to get ready and out the door. Try getting everyone up a half hour earlier to ease the morning stresses that often lead to conflict and can result in a parent/child disconnect.

February (Step 2)

Listen! ~ Once you've slowed down enough to breathe, it's time to stretch yourself and grow as a parent. Like most changes in life, it won't come easy, but the rewards are well worth it. Fred Rogers said, "Listening is where love begins," meaning that when we listen, we really get to know someone, learn about what motivates them, and understand their thoughts, hopes, dreams, hurts, disappointments, etc. All behaviors communicate underlying needs, and what we learn about the inner life of our children by listening to them will help us to focus on the needs behind the behaviors instead of simply correcting the 'symptoms' (i.e. the behavior).

As a parent, it may seem instinctive to insist that our children listen to us so that our guidance and/or correction can be heard. In fact, the number one complaint I get from most parents is, "My children just don't listen!" to which I respond, "Do you?"

The reality is that if a child doesn't feel they are being heard, then even if they stand silently 'listening' while we lecture or rant or even just talk, the child is simply rehearsing in their brain what they want to say rather than actually doing any effective listening. As the only adults in the parent/child relationship, it's up to the parent to be the first to listen, to *really* listen, because we are the ones with the maturity and self-control to be able to patiently wait to be heard.

March (Step 3)

Live what you want them to learn! ~ Ralph Waldo Emerson said, "What you do speaks so loud that I cannot hear what you say." Consciously, intentionally, and consistently living out how you want your children to turn out is the most powerful and effective character training there is. If you want your children to be kind, be kind. If you want them to be respectful, respect them. If you want them to learn self-control, model self-control. If you want them to be compassionate, treat them with compassion. If you want them to feel joy, enjoy them. If you want them to feel valuable, treasure them. The bottom line is, your children are always watching and learning, so make sure what they see in you is what you want to see in them!

April (Step 4)

Breathe! ~ We all get overwhelmed by the seemingly endless demands of life at times, so this month remind yourself to relax and consciously focus on enjoying your children. It's just a fact of human nature that when we enjoy something, we pay more attention to it, value it, and treat it better. Applying that fact to parenting, it makes sense to be intentional about taking time to laugh and hug and simply be with our children. Check out the 'bucket list' in chapter 15 of *Two Thousand Kisses a Day: Gentle Parenting Through the Ages and Stages* full of ideas for simple, memorable fun to share with life's most precious treasures, your children!

May (Step 5)

Book it! ~ It's been said that our treasure lies where our time, attention, and love is invested. While having special family outings and activities is a wonderful way to enjoy our children, it is in the daily routines and busyness of life that the parent/child connection can often suffer the most. One of the best ways to stay connected with our children is to build time into each day to invest in them, and one of the best investments is in a love of reading. A love of reading is born on the lap of a parent, in the soothing cadence of a mother's voice reading the same beloved story night after night, in the rhythmic sway of a rocking chair, and in the comfortable rustle of well-worn pages being turned one after another after another. A quiet bedtime routine that includes a nighttime story will not only help bedtime to be happier and smoother, but will also incorporate vital time for you to reconnect with your children at the end of every day.

June (Step 6)

Turn your no's into yes's! ~ In any home, like in any civilized society, boundaries are necessary for everyone's safety and comfort. With gentle parenting, setting limits focuses on connection and empathetic communication rather than control and punitive consequences. This month try setting limits using gentle parenting by turning your *no's* into *yes's*. Instead of *"No, you can't have ice cream until after dinner,"* try *"I know you love ice cream. I do, too! We're getting ready to eat right now, but what flavor would you like after dinner?"* This invites cooperation instead of triggering opposition, another hallmark of gentle parenting.

July (Step 7)

Play! ~ They say that the family that plays together, stays together, and there's great truth to that. Play is the language of childhood, and through play we get to know and connect with our children on their turf, in their native language, and on their terms. It's a powerful moment in a parent's life when they suddenly see their sweet little one as a separate, intelligent, worthy human being who can plan, make decisions, snap out orders, and lead other humans on a journey through an imaginary rainforest or on a trip through outer space. This month, try taking on the role of follower in your child's land of make-believe, and you'll discover a whole new world in which your child is strong, confident, and capable, and you'll come away with a deeper connection with and appreciation for the *person*, not just the child.

August (Step 8)

Eat well! ~ Along with all of the exercise you'll be getting playing with your child, take stock of the kinds of food you're providing to fuel their little engines and enrich their minds. Good nutrition may not be the first thought that pops into people's minds when they think of gentle parenting, but studies have shown that many behavior issues and sleep problems have their root in unhealthy eating habits, nutrient-poor diets, and food additives (dyes, preservatives, etc.). Children, especially littler ones, don't take change well as a general rule, and changes to the foods they eat are on top of the list of changes they'll resist. As a gentle parent, working with, instead of against, our children will help to make eating healthy a fun family project instead of a food fight. Try letting your children help you make weekly menus and shop for the fresh ingredients you'll be using, and let them help you cook, too. If they feel like they are a part of the change instead of a victim of it, they're far more likely to cooperate. If you have picky eaters, don't hesitate to serve them the same foods you normally do, just with a few added healthy ingredients slipped in to make them healthier. For ideas on ways to make healthy changes more fun, check out chapter 9 of *Two Thousand Kisses a Day: Gentle Parenting Through the Ages and Stages*.

September (Step 9)

Don't forget your funny bone! ~ Often the best parenting advice is simply, *"Chill out! Relax! Laugh a little, for goodness' sake!"* Sometimes as parents we get so caught up in 'fixing' our children that all we see are problems. We start focusing so much on preparing our children for their future that we forget to let them live in the present. One of the main problems with that is that children are, by their very nature, creatures of the 'now,' living fully immersed in each present moment. This month, pull out your dusty, old funny-bone, the one that used to keep you in stitches when you were a child, and laugh, on purpose, every day with your child. You'll be amazed at how a good belly laugh can turn even the worst day into something a little easier to handle and how much a giggle-fest can heal the little rifts that tend to occur in the parent/child connection throughout each day.

October (Step 10)

If you build it, they will come! ~ A shared project can offer a real chance to get to know your child on an entirely new level, so this month find something to build together. Choose something they are interested in, whether it's a model rocket or tree fort, and watch them blossom as they learn and build and grow. Your role is supportive--finding the materials, helping to read the instructions, offering suggestions or help when they struggle, etc. Simply being there through the process will enrich your connection with your child and offer you valuable insights into their interests and learning style, which will provide tools for you to use when helping them with their homework or if you are homeschooling them.

November (Step 11)

Gratitude is an attitude! ~ Teaching our children to be grateful involves far more than simply instructing them to say, *"Thank you."* We all want to be appreciated, and children are no different. Remember, modeling the things we want to see in our children is the single most powerful mode of instruction, so living a life of gratitude ourselves goes a long way toward raising our little ones to be happy, grateful humans. Openly appreciating our children, telling them what we like about them, and thanking them for the things they do is a sure-fire way of inspiring an attitude of gratitude in their little hearts. This month, be intentional in finding things to praise in your children. Don't be falsely enthusiastic or use *"Good job!"* as a brush-off to get them to leave you alone. Instead, honestly tell them what you like about them. Tell them *"Thank you"* when they remember to brush their teeth without being told or help their little sister with her block tower. Let them know you think their artwork is beautiful and don't hesitate to give them a pat on the back for a job well done when they straighten their room. Remember, it is the hungry child, not the satisfied child, who craves food, and, in the same way, it is *unmet* needs that lead to attention seeking behaviors and *unspoken* approval that can create 'praise junkies' as the unpraised child seeks to fill the very human need we all have for validation.

December (Step 12)

Celebrate! ~ Take time this month to give yourself a pat on the back for working toward your goal of becoming a gentle parent. Congratulate yourself for all that you've accomplished and take stock of your successes as well as your failures. Don't focus on your mistakes. Simply learn from them, forgive yourself, and move forward. Look back at where you were as a parent a year ago and compare that to where you are now. Don't worry if you haven't come as far as you'd like. Remember to give yourself grace. Life is for living and learning and growing, and another year is about to start with a chance to move forward into a new beginning. Everything you've invested in your children in the last year has been worthwhile, and everything you'll invest in the coming years will build on the foundation you've begun. So take this month to celebrate *you* and to enjoy the return on your investment!

~~~~~~~

Do you see a theme throughout this gentle parenting '12-step program'? Getting to know and enjoy your children as individuals, intentionally focusing on building and maintaining a strong and healthy parent/child connection, and living what you want your children to learn are the bedrocks of gentle parenting. Walking through these steps, revisiting them when you find yourself struggling, and appreciating the incredible, miraculous gifts that each individual child brings into the world will keep you growing as a gentle parent day after day, month after month, year after year.

Live. Laugh. Love. Enjoy!

References:

1. "By the Ages: Behavior & Development of Children Pre-Birth through Eight"; K. Eileen Allen and Lynn R. Marotz; 2000

2. Onya Baby, . "Can babywearing eliminate the need for tummy time?." N.p., 04 02 2012. Web. Web. 15 Feb. 2013. <http://onyababy.com/blog/2012/02/can-babywearing-eliminate-the-need-for-tummy-time/>.

3. Dr. Acredolo, , and Dr. Goodwin. "Baby Signs - Research." Baby Signs. n.d. n. page. Web. 3 Jun. 2013. <https://www.babysigns.com/index.cfm?id=64>.

4. "Aladdin - Quotes." IMDb. Disn'ys Aladdin, 1992. Web. 3 Jun. 2013. <http://www.imdb.com/title/tt0103639/quotes>.

5. Kerns KA (2008). "Attachment in Middle Childhood". In Cassidy J, Shaver PR. Handbook of Attachment: Theory, Research and Clinical Applications. New York and London: Guilford Press. pp. 366–82.

6. The Holy Bible: New International Version, Zondervan; Proverbs 15:1

Made in the USA
Middletown, DE
27 April 2015